THE BALLAD OF BABY DOE

THE BALLAD OF BABY DOE

"I Shall Walk Beside My Love"

DUANE A. SMITH
with John Moriarty

UNIVERSITY PRESS OF COLORADO

© 2002 by the University Press of Colorado

Published by the University Press of Colorado
5589 Arapahoe Avenue, Suite 206C
Boulder, Colorado 80303

The University Press of Colorado is a cooperative publishing enterprise supported, in part, by Adams State College, Colorado State University, Fort Lewis College, Mesa State College, Metropolitan State College of Denver, University of Colorado, University of Northern Colorado, University of Southern Colorado, and Western State College of Colorado.

The paper used in this publication meets the minimum requirements of the American National Standard for Information Sciences—Permanence of Paper for Printed Library Materials. ANSI Z39.48-1992

Library of Congress Cataloging-in-Publication Data

Smith, Duane A.
    The ballad of Baby Doe : "I shall walk beside my love" / Duane A. Smith with John Moriarty.
        p. cm.
    Includes bibliographical references (p.) and index.
        ISBN 0-87081-658-6 (cloth : alk. paper) — ISBN 0-87081-659-4 (pbk. : alk. paper)
        1. Moore, Douglas, 1893–1969. Ballad of Baby Doe. I. Moriarty, John, 1930– II. Title.
        ML410.M7753 S65 2002
        782.1—dc21

                                                                        2001006773

Design by Daniel Pratt

11 10 09 08 07 06 05 04 03 02   10 9 8 7 6 5 4 3 2 1

to the women and men
who produced and performed in
The Ballad of Baby Doe
in Central City

CONTENTS

PREFACE

USIC HISTORIAN AND AUTHOR Gilbert
Chase, in the 1988 edition of his classic *America s
Music,* wrote, *"The Ballad of Baby Doe* is unquestionably the most successful grand opera by an American to deal with the historical past of the United States." Composer
Douglas Moore, in this opera, "made [his] strongest and most
lasting impression." Chase continued, "Working within a traditional framework of arias and set pieces," Moore "skillfully deployed
his musical resources for the best dramatic effects and delineation
of character."

Christopher Hatch in the *International Dictionary of Opera* concurred, crediting Moore with skillfully delineating each character's
nature. His score, Hatch applauded, "overflows with pieces of

American popular, so-called vernacular styles from a hundred-or-so years before. . . . In a masterful fashion Moore, together with John Latouche, simplified and mingled traditional ingredients in *The Ballad of Baby Doe.* It is a singers' opera that has memorable melodies, elements of spectacle, points of national and historical interest, including musical Americana, and time-honored characters and plot."

When I first saw *Baby Doe,* during its premier 1956 season at the Central City Opera House, I had no idea that it would hook me into a lifelong interest in the Tabors, mining, and Colorado history. Nor did I realize that through it I would gain an appreciation for opera; Douglas Moore could have asked for no more from one performance of his work (this was the first opera I had ever seen). Although I am unable professionally to analyze the opera as Chase and Hatch did, I can say that I gained a passion for *Baby Doe,* one that has carried down through the years. That passion, perhaps, makes this less than an objective study!

This study of *Baby Doe,* truly a labor of love, could not have been accomplished without the assistance of a large group of people. Many of these would qualify as "Doeheads," as fans of this opera have been nicknamed. The support of the Central City Opera House Association has been crucial in many ways, from opening their archives to providing photographs to offering encouragement and support. Jo Ann Sims and Heather Thorwald helped in a variety of ways, as did chairman of the board Daniel Ritchie. Nancy Brittain and Pelham Pearce offered good cheer throughout. The staffs of the Denver Public Library, Western History/Genealogy Department, and Colorado Historical Society were their usual professional and helpful selves.

Critical to capturing the opera as performed at Central City were interviews conducted with the people who sang in *Baby Doe* on that stage. Their enthusiastic willingness to be interviewed and their enjoyment in recalling their performances and Central City experiences infinitely enhanced this study and gave it a unique flavor. Without question, they added a significance it would not have attained otherwise. My heartfelt gratitude goes to two who particularly went far beyond what I had hoped, Leyna Gabriele and Brian Steele. To one and all my sincere thanks and heartfelt appreciation. Their names and contributions are found throughout the chapters.

Two friends deserve special mention and acknowledgment, along with deep gratitude for the help they provided. The original Doehead, David Kanzeg, whose love for this opera is unsurpassed, graciously provided his interviews with the Moore family, cast members, and others associated with *Baby Doe*. I have had the pleasure of working with John Moriarty, now artistic director emeritus of the Central City Opera, on several occasions. His professionalism, insights, and support have kept me going.

The staff of the University Press of Colorado has once again encouraged and supported my efforts. Special thanks are extended to Laura Furney, Daniel Pratt, David Archer, and former director Luther Wilson.

Finally, "three cheers and a tiger" to my wife, Gay, who has gone with me to every Central City *Baby Doe* season since 1956. Her editing and love have sustained not only this volume but all those that came before.

PROLOGUE
"Love Is Eternal"

A BRAHAM LINCOLN HAD "Love Is Eternal" inscribed on the wedding band he gave Mary Todd. Considering the trials and tribulations of their courtship and marriage, that indeed proved to be true. The same has been true for Central City, the Central City Opera House, the opera association, and its opera, *The Ballad of Baby Doe.*

Central City, or as early residents called it, "Central," for over a decade reigned as Colorado's premier mining town, a worthy rival of Denver. Its businesses, schools, and churches represented some of the finest in the territory, and its cosmopolitan population considered itself unmatched. The "Little Kingdom of Gilpin" relished in its heyday and pointed with pride to its "crown jewel," the opera house.

Central quickly settled down from its birth pangs and did not measure up to the rowdy, red-tinged images visitors had of mining towns even in the 1860s. It was, noted one 1870 writer, a town "not devoid" of the educational, religious, and literary institutions one expected to encounter in older eastern communities: "Nor is it behind in the fashions, follies and vices which follow civilization everywhere. The former is illustrated by substantial school buildings, churches, literary institutions and libraries; the latter by the appearance of fashionably and over-dressed ladies and gentlemen at public gatherings, and in the streets, and the same evidences of reckless living and dissipation which present themselves in every American city."

Central City had come of Victorian age. The Central Citians could not help but be pleased for they, like their western mining contemporaries, were striving to re-create the life they had left behind. At least they tried as it existed within their power to do so.

Only Denver rivaled Central City's political power during the territorial years, and Central's Henry Teller became one of the first two U.S. senators from the Centennial State. Central City's influence reached its peak in the 1870s, although its census population topped out in 1900 at slightly more than 3,000. Meanwhile, Central's mines produced at least a million dollars annually from 1867 through 1909, an outstanding record of production for a mining district. Although usually considered a gold district, Gilpin County produced silver, copper, lead, and zinc, in that monetary order.

All that was fine, but a mining town without an opera house seemed poor. Even the smaller and less wealthy mining camps aspired to have this apex of Victorian culture. Central had theaters in the 1860s but no imposing structure that would mark its coming of age. The very successful local production of *The Bohemian Girl* in the Belvedere Theater on April 17, 1877, created interest in a better theater. As a result, later that year a group of Central City folk formed the Gilpin County Opera House Association. They quickly moved to raise funds and build such a structure. On March 4, 1878, after spending $32,000, the grand opening heralded Central City's triumph. Noted Colorado architect, forty-four-year-old

Robert Roeschlaub, designed a building that would be "in harmony with the great mountains surrounding it, and an expression of the new and simple West." He succeeded. A glittering
audience of the Little Kingdom's society and Denverites who had
come up for the occasion greeted this magnificent tribute to the
spirit and pride of Central and Gilpin County.

For a brief, shining moment, Central City grabbed the crown
as Colorado's mining and cultural capital, but that crown rested
uneasily. The opening happened just as Leadville was about to
steal Central City's claim as the number one Colorado mining
town and district. Horace Tabor built an opera house for Leadville
and also one for Denver. Central's reign was over.

Opera might not have been played there much, because the
house more typically hosted plays, vaudeville, political rallies,
wrestling matches, lectures, high school graduations, and even
funerals. Thomas Hornsby Ferril, in his haunting poem "Magenta,"
about women in Central City, captured a glimpse of it.

> Each woman had seven children of whom two
> Were living, and the two would go to church.
> Sometimes the children went to the opera-house
> To see the tragedies. They can still remember
> The acrobats and buglers between the acts.

Although an opera house might represent a grand aspiration,
that did not translate into profit at the box office. Sadly, support
waned; the opera house never would be a moneymaker. The building was sold in 1882; it was almost converted into a courthouse
but was rescued at the last moment by public-spirited local citizens who reorganized the defunct opera house association. In the
depression-locked 1890s, times, the local economy, and interests
changed. That proved the final straw. The association finally gave
up and sold the opera house to Peter McFarlane in 1900.

In the new century, leisure activities became more varied. An
opera house could not match the popularity of that new wonder,
the movies. McFarlane realized this and converted his building
into a movie theater. Even that could not save it. With mining
and Central's steady, unrelenting decline, the now outdated movie

theater closed in 1927. The deteriorating and abandoned opera house was rescued in the early 1930s when public- and preservation-spirited women, Anne Evans and Ida McFarlane, acquired it. Both women had ties to pioneering families and Central City. Anne's father had been the second territorial governor, John Evans, and Ida had married into the McFarlane family with its extensive connection to the opera house.

On inspection, they sadly found a building in worse condition than they expected. They established what became the Central City Opera House Association and set to work. Plans for an early opening had to be dropped. Joined by, among others, Allen True—who headed the renovation committee and restored the murals himself—actress and patron of the arts Edna Chappell, and Denver architect Allen Fisher, they set about to raise funds and restore the building. Edna, with her strong theatrical interests, was also instrumental in the early theatrical productions in the opera house she did so much to save.

Despite being in the throes of America's worst depression, with hard work and innovations, such as "selling" the hickory chairs by having pioneers pay $100 to have their names inscribed on the backs, the funds were raised and the work was completed. The first festival opened in 1932. (The Central City summer season has long been called a festival and for years included a play at the end of the opera.) The *Rocky Mountain News* headline (July 17, 1932) trumpeting that occasion informed its readers, "Central City Roars Wide Open in Revival of Old Mining Days." For a moment, the festivities that night offered an opportunity to forget the deepening depression that engulfed the town, state, nation, and world.

Only twenty-four years divided that sparkling evening and the opening of *The Ballad of Baby Doe.* A blink in history, it nonetheless represented the survival, success, and coming-of-age of the revived Central City Opera House.

BABY DOE
COMES OF AGE
The Making of an Opera

What's the matter, Fogarty, ain't my money good enough? Lamp this lovely silver ore! Got a right to celebrate, found a peerless matchless mine—I call it the Matchless Mine, got a right to raise some Hell, silver oozing from the soil—yippee!

ON SATURDAY EVENING, JULY 7, 1956, the curtain rose on the world premiere of *The Ballad of Baby Doe* at the Central City Opera House. Before the curtain went up that expectant evening and the old miner sang these opening lines, *Baby Doe* had traveled a steep and rocky road much like the Colorado mining era it portrayed. Those earlier days of the opera had given it some of the tribulations all three Tabors had endured in real life.

Three forces came together to give birth to *The Ballad of Baby Doe*. Initially, the appealing nature of the story itself beckoned. It was one of Colorado's most endearing sagas. The second involved the curiosity of composer Douglas Moore. He had been attracted to the story of Baby Doe when he read the account of her death in

1935 at the Matchless Mine. The third, and what proved the para-
mount mover, was the Central City Opera House Association's
interest.

At least some members of the association's board were interested in commissioning an opera with an American setting. A
pioneering Colorado mining family seemed the perfect choice for
a subject when they discussed the topic in 1953. The key player in
the unfolding drama was the association's president, fifty-eight-
year-old Frank Ricketson Jr., who had succeeded founder Anne
Evans as the second president in 1943. The gracious and imposing Ricketson (Rick as he was known) was one of Denver's leading philanthropists and a man well schooled in the world of show
business. The owner of a chain of movie houses (Fox Intermoun-
tain Theaters) in Denver and the surrounding region, he had successfully operated and marketed them during the Depression. For
two decades he guided the fortunes of the association.

Ricketson told the board it should enlarge the scope of its
activities because the novelty had "disappeared from the festivals."
A motion came up at the November 2 meeting to commission
Paul Green and Douglas Moore "to collaborate in the creation
of an original opera dealing with the life and times of Baby Doe
and Horace W. Tabor" to be presented at Central City in 1955.
The motion failed. The terse minutes gave no clue as to why.
More than likely the hesitancy reflected the lack of success, financially and critically, of the 1935 production *Central City Nights.*
The association commissioned that work and lost money; unfortunately, the association board had a long memory. Perhaps the
vague commission "price of between $5,000 and $10,000" forced
a reconsideration. Financial considerations always weighed heavily
with the association.

Another problem emerged and probably influenced the vote.
The association was losing money on the seasonal operas at Central City. Only the play, offered after the opera season, kept the
income and expense gap from widening to an alarming figure.
Could it afford to gamble on an operatic innovation?

For whatever reason or reasons, attitudes changed. At the
December 2 meeting, with Ricketson's persuasive influence spear-

heading the effort, the board gave permission to negotiate with Green and Moore. This time both men were to be offered a "fee" between $5,000 and $10,000. Negotiations started immediately, and by the January 11, 1954, board meeting, the association had reached a "tentative understanding" on a contract. Green and Moore were to receive $5,000 each for an opera, with a full performance time of "approximately two hours." Rick's influence surfaced again. A feature-length movie ran about that same amount of time! The opera had to be ready to be produced during summer of 1955.

Then the board members made a decision that would come back to haunt them. "It was unanimously decided that Miss Caroline Bancroft be made historical advisor" to Moore and Green in their "work on the Tabor opera." It was "to be understood that this position carries no remuneration nor does it entitle Miss Bancroft to any rights or benefits from the production." Caroline, however, was not going to see it quite that way.

Miss Bancroft did not remember the conversation that way: "Oh Goodness no—that was not what we agreed, if my memory serves." She wanted an honorarium because she held "five copyrights to various phases of the Tabor material." Fascinating enough, she claimed to have copyrighted the name *Baby Doe!* Following that flight of fancy, Caroline contacted her lawyers for advice.

The three turned out to be a most intriguing, if not harmonious, troika. Sixty-one-year-old composer Douglas Moore, "a warm and charming man," had long used Americana as an artistic resource. His Pulitzer Prize–winning folk opera, *The Devil and Daniel Webster* (1939), was much admired and already considered by some critics to be a classic. Moore had realized that a tuneful, popular style proved ideally suited to depict American events, and he was fascinated by, as previously mentioned, the Tabor story. North Carolinian Paul Green, author and former university professor, was well-known for a variety of publications, including plays, movie scripts, and books. He had won a Pulitzer Prize in 1927 for the play *In Abraham s Bosom.* The third-generation Colorado writer and historian Caroline Bancroft had already written on the Tabors. They were to her a prized personal possession in which she owned a strong "proprietary interest." Caroline could be counted on to guard the "holy grail" with a stubborn determination. As one person observed, "She was a woman of rather formidable mien and noted for speaking her mind." That proved an understatement!

The opening volley of what became an obstinate fight, to the disgust (if not horror) of the board, came in a letter from Bancroft on January 30, 1954. It was typically Caroline. She opened: "Please excuse the delay but I have been in Aspen all week, doing the kind of primary research, in the field, which makes my work unique in that realm of Colorado history. We are and have been over-run by that sort of Eastern writer who stays thirty-six hours in Colorado and is then an authority!" Apparently, by this time the board had offered her an "honorarium" of $250, and when her lawyer approved, she tendered, "I will be delighted to accept."

Caroline commented in a January 30, 1954, letter that she had been in contact with Paul Green, who had read her Baby Doe pamphlet, "Silver Queen," and obviously wanted to "dramatize it." The two had a luncheon meeting that proved "disquieting" because he had quoted from her work and claimed it was in the public domain. She did say, "I thought your [Ricketson's] great executive ability and capacity to handle delicate situations would bridge a certain misapprehension that Mr. Green has on what constitutes 'public domain.'" With that opening shot, in February she retired to talk to her lawyer: "You know that it is always my preference to be constructive and helpful."

In February 1954 she declared she wanted 2 percent of the "gross receipts of any eventual production," an honorarium of $500, and credits for being "the Tabor authority of the world." That proved too much for Ricketson, who wrote Caroline on March 1, 1954, that if "we cannot agree," this correspondence will be terminated and "our discussion brought to a conclusion."

Meanwhile, the Executive Committee was meeting with the attorney for Moore and Green regarding the contract. Such matters as the size of the orchestra, the authors' expenses for attending rehearsals, and the quality of the production had to be resolved.

They hammered out whatever troubled them and sent a contract back to New York.

Then came another volley. Moore "couldn't use" Green's libretto "to write his opera." He concluded that it was "unusable for his purposes." The harassed Ricketson hurried off to New York in late March for a discouraging meeting. Moore and his lawyer suggested Green "be paid off; that is, that he receive a few hundred dollars reimbursement for his expenses." Moore would then arrange for another librettist with an advance of $1,000.

The beleaguered Ricketson then met with an outside reader who agreed with Moore's conclusion "that you couldn't write an opera from that composition that Mr. Green was furnishing." Unable to contact Green or his lawyer, the association, through Ricketson, finally told Moore that if Green would drop out and settle "for a few hundred dollars," they could go ahead with the project.

Ricketson continued on to Washington, where Green finally contacted him. Green claimed he was a dramatist, not a historian. He feared the dramatic structure would "suffer in deference to the facts." Poor Ricketson saw his dream of a Colorado opera vanishing.

Green countered that he was not satisfied with Moore's previous operas. Most intriguing, Paul announced that the Tabor story belonged to him. Now he would like to hire his own composer and produce the show in New York City when it was completed. Having finished (Green claimed) three-fourths of a book, he figured he had put in too much time to drop out now. He said the subject was very active in his mind, that he had been "living" some of the scenes, and that the story belonged to him to finish.

Bancroft jumped back into the fray with a barrage of letters. She continued to claim she had uncovered a great many "hitherto unknown facts" about Baby Doe. They were hers and hers alone! Caroline wanted to collaborate on the opera's libretto because Green, or any librettist for that matter, would be using material that could only have been "obtained" from her booklets—material Bancroft asserted she had "copyrighted." Green had made a "fatal" mistake; he had used her material without crediting

Bancroft. As opera critic/reviewer Allen Young, who watched matters develop, laughingly said, "It got to be a really hot situation because only Caroline Bancroft knew what Baby Doe was thinking at specific times!"

Green refuted Caroline's claims, asserting correctly that he had not infringed on Bancroft's "domain" and that every fact he used existed in the public domain. The Tabors were public figures. A reading of Green's story outline supports his contention. Caroline, however, rebutted with a threatened lawsuit if anybody used her material. Caroline had planted "her flag firmly on the mound of research surrounding the Tabors."

Since these were real people and their lives a part of the history of Colorado and the West, Bancroft stood on—at best— shaky legal ground. Her counterargument, that her booklets were more "story" than history or biography, proved more truthful than people realized at the time. Bancroft had a "good many" friends in Denver, however, so it behooved the association not to ignore her.

The spring of discontent fastened on the association, with less than a year to go before the opera was to be completed. As might be imagined and understood, the once enthusiastic Ricketson grew disillusioned with the project. Green's and Moore's ideas remained so completely different that it seemed they could never reconcile them. Each man appeared disenchanted with the other and his earlier efforts at writing and composing. Green's story outline, a copy of which is in existence, did not live up to his claim of "living" some of the scenes. It dragged and appeared more hackneyed than lively and captivating.

Moore also became "very upset" with Bancroft and the threatened lawsuit. The association, as can easily be envisioned, neared the point of wanting no part of the besieged Tabor opera. The situation looked bleak.

Poor Rick became almost despondent. After his trip back East, he reported to the association:

> After talking with Mr. Green, whose ideas were so entirely different from Mr. Moore's, I came to the conclusion that I was being included in a deal that I wanted no part of. I did not wish to appraise the abilities of Mr. Green to write a

libretto or of Mr. Moore to write an opera and, if they
couldn't get along, our association certainly wanted no part
of it. I so notified Messrs. Douglas Moore and Paul Green.

Ricketson's well-known "business acumen and charm" were being stressed to the limit.

The Central Opera House Association minutes go strangely
silent (only two mentions between May 3, 1954, and June 21,
1955) about the future of the Tabor opera. At that point Green's
role in the story ended, but not before he threatened to sue the
association. Completely at odds with Moore and Bancroft, faced
with a potential lawsuit himself, and under attack from several
directions, Green had to go or there would be no opera. The
association dissolved the agreement, probably with a payout.

A new librettist was found, the young and rising writer John
Latouche. The escalating expenses and turmoil, however, nearly
proved too much. The association was ready to relinquish its role
in the production when Moore stepped in and approached the
Koussevitzky Foundation in search of funds. Moore had previously contacted the foundation about support, but it had been
unable at that time to offer enough financial patronage. This time
the foundation agreed to fund the cost of completing the libretto
and paying Latouche. Therefore, Koussevitzky received credit when
the opera was performed and recorded, which was done "under
the auspices" of the foundation.

The Koussevitzky Foundation entered the picture at a point
when the Central City Opera House Association faced a serious
cash flow problem. Having spent more money than anticipated at
this time in the opera's development, the association had reached
a crisis. And it had no opera to show for all the money spent and
the past months' stress.

In reality, however, the crisis had passed. The foundation
would commission the newly rejuvenated project to honor Columbia University's bicentennial (Moore taught there), while Central City would retain the right to stage the world premiere. The
opera saga would go on.

Moore and Latouche complemented each other perfectly. Yet,
as their mutual friend Jack Beeson observed, "They were an odd

John Latouche, Douglas Moore, Emerson Buckley, and Hanya Holm discuss Baby Doe. *Courtesy, Central City Opera House Association*

couple, but odd couples can make good opera!" In fact Latouche, a popular writer who had recently worked with Leonard Bernstein on *Candide,* had suggested to Moore that they write an opera together. They were opposites in some ways, even physically; Moore was tall, whereas Latouche was short and pudgy. Latouche, with an earthy charisma, with a bit of a roguish nature, contrasted with the "patrician" yet charming Moore.

As Allen Young wrote in *Opera in Central City* (1993), Latouche brought to the collaboration the feeling of a dramatic pulse that Moore admired. "More importantly," he continued, John provided "exactly the sentimental center which the two handkerchief opera needed." Moore, who had been praised for his easy lyrical style and his ability to work with "folk" themes, provided a perfect match. Moore later commented in an interview in *Time* (July 16, 1956), "I tried to return to melody as the key communication."

With the composer/librettist conflict resolved, work went ahead. The relieved Ricketson, who still deeply believed in the project, actually advanced money personally for the opera's completion. Ricketson was pleased to report in September 1954 that he had seen Moore in New York and "good progress was being made on the Tabor Opera." He was realistic, though, in doubting "that Mr. Moore would be able to have the opera finished in time for the 1955 festival." The annual report for 1954 announced that the new date for completion of the opera was fall of 1955. The opera premiere was changed to 1956.

The report also stated for all to read that the association had not "commission[ed] either the composer or the librettist." Furthermore, it would consider producing the opera "only after it is assured that it meets the high standards of our annual productions." The admission that the Koussevitzky Foundation had entered the picture and the association did not have full rights to the opera shocked some of its members.

Latouche had been, as he said initially in *Theatre Arts* (July 1956), "a trifle hesitant" because he felt nostalgic American historical plays and musicals had not been overwhelmingly successful: "A trip to the library for research, and my first contact with the real story, suddenly shook me awake." Latouche and Moore vigorously set to work.

John Latouche, writing in 1956 just before the opera debuted, remembered those days as less hectic than they may have seemed from Central City and Denver: "After some preliminary discussion, I was requested to do the libretto. The Koussevitzky Foundation commissioned Dr. Moore and myself to write the opera." He did indicate some pressure when he noted that the "last note of the orchestration was put down on April 1, 1956."

By March 1955 Moore was far enough along that Frank Ricketson had heard the first act. He was "favorably impressed," as he told the association's Executive Committee. By fall, enough progress had been made that New York and local committees were appointed to study the "Tabor Opera" score and submit written reports. Then came the crucial October 14 meeting, at which Moore appeared.

He played the opera score for members of the committee and "sang a good many of the parts." Moore outlined the opera's story and the "general scheme of the presentation." The committee then moved to present *The Ballad of Baby Doe* as one of the two operas for the 1956 season. The members' belief that *Baby Doe* was probably "the finest American folk opera that has ever been written" raised spirits throughout the association.

Apparently they did not finalize the name, for at the next meeting two weeks later it was decided that the opera, *Saga of Baby Doe,* would be presented sixteen times during the festival. After discussing various titles, the board reached no final conclusion. Sometime during the next two weeks they made the decision, and *The Ballad of Baby Doe* had found its name. During October the board also discussed setting the opening night main-floor ticket price at ten dollars. With the committee's overwhelmingly enthusiastic report, matters in the November and December meetings moved along energetically. The contract for the next season had been signed, individuals were suggested for various roles and for director, and the association agreed to pay the expenses of preparing the score. It also retained the right to rent "said scores." Emerson Buckley was engaged as musical director for the 1956 season. Always cautious, the Executive Committee "hoped that the total cost of casting" would not exceed $20,000.

The upcoming season would be Central City's twenty-fifth, and the 1955 Annual Report cited the progress made.

For the early years in Central City, management could herald the romantic experiences that awaited a trip to a nearby ghost mining town which blossomed three weeks in the summer. That has long since ceased to be exciting: the cycle when novelty was an asset to the Central City Festivals has ended.

There is no longer selling novelty in a trip to Central. When one purchases a theatre ticket one expects to see the finest professional performance in America.

Central City is expected to have the same quality ingredients or fundamentals and characteristics as the Metropolitan, Glyndebourne and Salzburg.

Concerning the opera house and *Baby Doe,* the report concluded, "We are part of a movement, if not a crusade. We seek to build upon our enduring monument to Colorado's pioneers. We strive for quality in our colorful, historic surroundings."

That said, the Executive Committee still worriedly discussed *Baby Doe.* The members awarded the contract for the set and costumes, with an optional clause to purchase the costumes "should *Baby Doe* prove to be a hit." At the January 25, 1956, meeting, they again discussed "at length various other names that might be used in place of *The Ballad of Baby Doe.*" They decided to retain "the present nomenclature," at least until "a more suitable title could be found—if any." At that meeting it was determined "that no credit should be given Caroline Bancroft by the Association in the matter of billing for *Baby Doe.*"

Caroline had not been a factor since March 1954. Her high-toned attitude as "the leading Tabor authority" had diminished to the point that she beggingly wrote Rick in November 1955, wondering if the position of historical adviser "is still open." He wrote back that the Koussevitzky Foundation had taken the matter out of the association's hands, adding: "I realize this subject is very, very dear to your heart and I would like to see you associated with the enterprise in some way." It would not happen. A threatened lawsuit and a $500 payment ended her involvement in the project.

By the January 25, 1956, Executive Committee meeting, contracts had been tendered for various roles, and the casting was soon completed, along with the selection of professional staff. In the months that followed, incidentals—such as sponsoring a reception "for cast, press, and other celebrities" after the world premiere—were completed.

Advance ticket sales went well, outpacing the companion opera, *La Tosca,* by nearly a third. Planning proceeded vigorously for the opening night festivities. United Airlines, for example, provided transportation for "certain Music Critics." To bypass federal regulations against airlines providing free transportation, the company made a contribution "to the Association in the amount equal to the cost of such transportation." The Brown Palace agreed

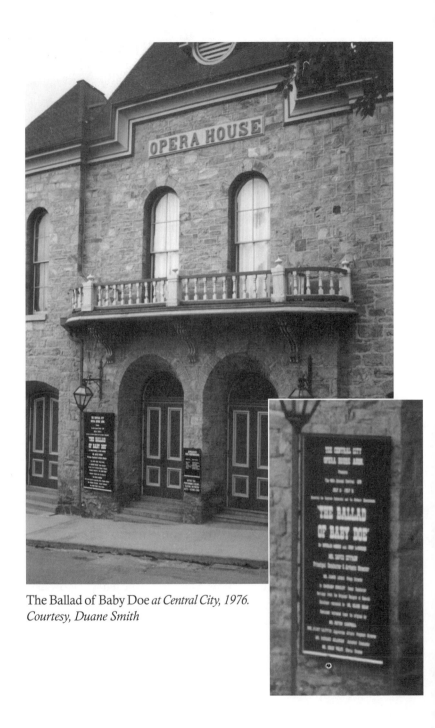

The Ballad of Baby Doe *at Central City, 1976.*
Courtesy, Duane Smith

to provide "at no cost . . . rooms, food, liquor, stationery and other items" and also to host a gala dinner party and a private reception following the debut. An intensive television-radio promotion was mapped out, and special sections in the *Denver Post* and the *Rocky Mountain News* were drafted for late June.

In the meantime, the cast assembled and rehearsals started. The intent was to have two artists sing each of the leading characters in alternate performances. That, plus teaching some very inexperienced young singers to dance and act, resulted in numerous long rehearsals.

Latouche attended few rehearsals, although, as co-director Edwin Levy commented, "he certainly listened and watched very attentively those he did attend. Occasionally, he would make a suggestion about staging, but he rarely intruded upon our rehearsal plans." Writing about this period in the July 1956 *Theatre Arts,* Latouche generously passed around compliments about the final weeks before the premiere: "I feel that together we [Donald Oenslager, designer; Emerson Buckley, conductor; and Hanya Holm and Ed Levy, co-directors] have animated a compelling section of American history." Oenslager played more of a role than simply that of an outstanding set designer; he is given credit for the suggestion to "bring in" Moore in the first place. Latouche and Moore had been "vastly aided by the suggestions" of these people.

Not all went so smoothly. Buckley, a former student of Moore's at Columbia, was "determined to have an exciting performance." Not unexpectedly, rehearsals did not always go as he hoped, and Buckley often "lost his temper," one person remembered. Holm and Levy proved a perfect team. A leading "exponent of the dance," Holm had never done opera, whereas Levy had extensive operatic directing experience. Holm choreographed, and Levy handled the operatic aspects.

Douglas Moore, in a *New York Times* article on July 1, described his feelings about the opera whose characters jumped out of history. The "dramatic and touching story" made an "ideal outline for an opera libretto." Discussing the problem of having to "invent" some scenes, he focused on Augusta, concluding that

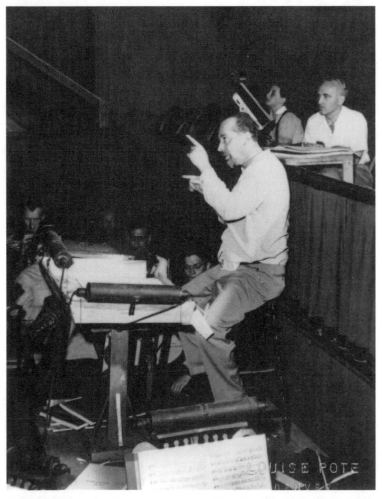

Emerson Buckley conducting a rehearsal in 1956. Courtesy, Central City Opera House Association

"we could not afford to give up such an interesting character." Augusta in real life dropped out of Horace's life immediately after the divorce, but that was not the case in the opera. One of the most difficult points was portraying the gap between Tabor's death and that of Baby Doe thirty-six years later. In some detail, Moore

The cozy and intimate Central City Opera House. Courtesy, Mark Kiryluk

discussed how he and Latouche handled the problem. Overall, the article teased the reader enough to stir interest in *Baby Doe,* which was already being discussed for a possible New York opening.

Caroline Bancroft briefly resurfaced in the preparations, meeting Latouche to go over the final libretto. Latouche had handled Caroline the right way—meeting with her, flattering her, and saying he wanted to "do her justice." After suggesting a few minor changes, she observed, "Now it is a good script." Moore jokingly remarked, "It really is an opera. I hope that doesn't frighten anyone."

With a dash of tribulation and boundless expectations, the "dreaded day" approached. A few more "bugs" needed to be worked out in the final rehearsals. Then the day arrived. The world premiere, July 7, 1956, was received with "unprecedented enthusiasm," according to the pleased association. Leyna Gabriele, one of the two Baby Does that season, was there that evening: "There was a lot of excitement attendant to this, as you can imagine; you know, there was a world premiere, there were photographers and lots of people. Particularly since it was an opera where characters had lived and had been in this actual town, it was really a very exciting time." She went on to say, "It was wonderful to be a part of it, and having been part from the very beginning was even more exciting for me."

The next day both the *Denver Post* and the *Rocky Mountain News* saluted the opera. The *News* headline enthusiastically proclaimed, "*Ballad of Baby Doe* Is Smash Hit: First-Nighters Cheer." *Post* music columnist Allen Young was more restrained: "*Baby Doe* praised as forceful, original."

"Composer Douglas Moore and librettist John Latouche have reached another peak in American opera in skillful collaboration on *Baby Doe*. It is a great achievement," wrote delighted *News* critic Robert Smith. He praised everything from the "magnificent score" to the "beautiful, brilliant and at times most daring costumes, sets, and lighting" and, finally, the "thrilling performance." He did not ignore the cast. He hailed the "superb" Walter Cassel as Tabor, the "natural" Dolores Wilson as Baby Doe, and Martha Lipton, who "literally sang her heart out and gave a most memorable performance," as Augusta.

The *Post* echoed these sentiments and praised the Central City Opera House Association for its "courage and determination to make possible this venture and their rightness in choosing to make *The Ballad of Baby Doe* their first American opera." If possible, the review soared even higher in its comments about the three leading artists—Wilson, Lipton, and Cassel—"a trio of principals whose unerring feeling for the role brings such strength to the performance." As many others commented later, Young noted that the audience was "initially charmed, then deeply moved" by this story of three people "weathering summery joys and wintry sorrows in the Colorado of an earlier day as they meet their destinies."

New York Times (July 9, 1956) reviewer Howard Taubman was impressed with Moore and Latouche's "old-fashioned sentiment redolent of the era of crinolines . . . and the innocent Western

Horace and Baby Doe meet at the Clarendon Hotel in 1956. Courtesy, Central City Opera House Association

urge for respectability and 'culture.'" Holm and Levy were praised for staging the work "with gusto and theatrical effectiveness" and Buckley for conducting with "authority and understanding of an American theme. . . . Taken all in all, *The Ballad of Baby Doe* is a tender, sentimental evocation of the past with the character of Augusta providing the redeeming bite that gives it dimension as art."

In a follow-up article (July 15, 1956), Taubman focused more on the town and festival than on the opera, and his comments seemed more reserved. He described the musical idiom as "conventional" and said the tunes lacked "profile and intensity," yet at the same time he praised the opera's admirable "attention to detail." Although he questioned whether it would be viable on other stages, Taubman thought *Baby Doe* was "good and right for Central City."

Curtain call, opening night 1956. Courtesy, Central City Opera House Association

In its July 16, 1956, issue, *Time* applauded Moore, Latouche, and *Baby Doe*: "Out of this invitingly gaudy material [Tabor story] composer Moore has wrought a clean, melodious score which succeeds in conveying strong period flavor without being condescendingly folksy." The review continued, "Sophisticated musically, the score nevertheless is marked by a clarity rare to the U. S. Opera stage." *Life* (August 6, 1956) presented the opera in photographs. In an interesting sequence, the article presented a photographic comparison of the Tabors with their operatic counterparts. At this point Caroline struck again. She claimed those were her photographs and sued *Life*. The story goes that the magazine paid her two or three hundred dollars to settle the matter.

Emmy Rogers, in *Musical America* (August 1956), called *Baby Doe* the "season's most discussed musical event." She praised

Latouche's "fine feeling for the theatre" and his boldly drawn characterizations. Composer Moore was lauded for the music, which was "colorful, yet unobtrusive, and [which] catches the era's atmosphere with a mixture of nostalgia and rugged harmonies." Rogers felt Moore had "given Augusta the opera's best music," a debate that continues among Doeheads." Does Augusta or Baby Doe carry the day? That question has rebounded down the years and through various performances.

Charles Johnson, in *Opera in the Rockies,* recalled Albert Goldberg's *Los Angeles Times* review as less complimentary. He felt the major dramatic scenes were more theatrical than musical. Moore's music, he believed, underlined the lighter moments much more "deftly than [it] scaled the dramatic heights." Allen Young, in a September 1999 interview, vividly remembered one review. Apparently bothered by Moore's and Latouche's rejection of "currently fashionable musical devices," Roger Dettmer, in the *Chicago American,* decided they "had produced a mouse."

Overall, however, the reviews were excellent. Certainly, the local reviews might have been expected to be favorable, but as the *Rocky Mountain News* reported on July 8, 1956, much of the national coverage nearly mirrored the "tumultuous, frenzied applause, the cheers and bravos" of the first-nighters.

The acceptance battle, nonetheless, was far from won. Commenting on the opera after viewing a New York production, an eastern critic later dismissed it as "musical comedy claimed for the opera house" (*New Yorker,* May 10, 1976). The unnamed reviewer continued to proclaim that what made *Baby Doe* a bore was "the blandness of its melodies—cliché tunes accompanying, not bringing vividness and particularity to, a play that is itself a series of dramatic clichés." A dose of eastern elitism and snobbishness could be sensed throughout the review.

Latouche, in concluding his article in *Theatre Arts,* wrote about his experiences with *Baby Doe,* stating that the "making has been a memorable and rewarding experience." He wondered about the opera's reception: "Its interest for an audience, naturally, remains to be seen." That test of time has passed forty years, and *Baby Doe* has grown in stature and following. The nay-saying critics have

John Moriarty conducting Baby Doe. *Courtesy, Central City Opera House Association*

been proven wrong. The Tabors have not been forgotten "like a whisper in the wind."

Before the 1956 season, treasurer Davis Moore had worried that the production of an original opera would "commit itself [the association] to unknown but substantial financial obligation." He and others had been concerned that "most original works fail in their first presentation." He need not have fretted. His 1956 report summarized the story of *Baby Doe*'s success: "I believe that every member of the Association can be extremely proud that the production of *The Ballad of Baby Doe* was not only enthusiastically received and attended, but as far as I am able to determine, was the only major original Opera ever undertaken on a professional level to which every ticket to every performance was sold before the curtain rose. Moreover, it was necessary to add additional performances."

NOT COMPLETELY SATISFIED WITH THEIR OPERA, Moore and Latouche determined to make several changes, which were fin-

Leyna Gabriele, one of the two Baby Does in the original production, and Douglas Moore. Courtesy, Leyna Gabriele

ished just before the latter's death in August 1956. Believing Tabor's character needed to be strengthened, they replaced an aria with the love song in Act I, Scene 2, "Warm as the Autumn Light," and the new scene in Act II, Scene 2, where Horace plays poker with his four friends. Douglas wanted that scene to parallel the one of Augusta and the four "gossips." Eliminating an interlude of children's games tightened the scene involving Bryan at Leadville. They gave Baby Doe a new aria, "The Fine Ladies Walk" (Act II, Scene 1), to replace one called "Wake Snakes." A critic said "thank goodness" to the disappearance of the first production's least memorable aria.

There is also a mystery. Part of the original score, just before the opening scene with the old miner and Matchless Mine, has been lost. It included a square dance.

The Ballad of Baby Doe has gained respect and admiration over the years from the public and critics alike. Allen Young's words the evening of the premiere are as true today as they were then: "In its re-creation of the spirit of a different age the production finds the way to speak vividly in bright color and song."

Young made an interesting observation in a 1999 interview about *Baby Doe*: "it's kind of a tragic opera, but without villains." He went on to say, "Both Baby Doe and Augusta are made to seem like very strong and really admirable people who may not have always been honorable in their actions but were basically admirable. Tabor is made to seem a very sympathetic character." Concluding, he observed, "So there really aren't any villains in the opera, which is, I think, quite an achievement."

Villains, no; a love story, yes. This timeless love story has become the eternal opera of an epic Colorado era. Arguably the most beautiful and moving aria in the opera captures this abiding spirit. As she stands, framed by the Matchless Mine with snow falling on her, Baby Doe sings:

> Never shall the mourning dove
> Weep for us in accents wild
> I shall walk beside my love
> Who is husband, father, child.
>
> As our earthy eyes grow dim
> Still the old song will be sung.
> I shall change along with him
> So that both are ever young.
>
> Ever young.

THE TABORS
A Legendary Story

IN THE FINAL SCENE OF *The Ballad of Baby Doe,* an old and tired Horace Tabor reviews his life as he stands on the stage of Denver's Tabor Grand Opera House. Augusta, a ghostly shape in his mind's eye, confronts him: "You are going to die, Horace Tabor, and you die a failure." The opera and Tabor then pose the question that has echoed down the years and into the twenty-first century: How does one assess a man and his era? They have faded into history along with their values, their aspirations, and generational pressures. As a contemporary and onetime Nevada silver miner, Sam Clemens (better known later as Mark Twain) revealed, "I was young then, marvelously young then, wonderfully young, younger than ever again by several hundred years."

Tabor, in one of the revealing and touching moments of the emotional last scene, attempts to answer that question. Actually, he provides insights for all who hope to understand and appreciate his times.

> How can a man measure himself?
> The land was growing, and I grew with it.
> In my brain rose buildings yearning towards the sky,
> And my guts sank deep in the plunging mineshafts
> My feet kicked up gold dust wherever I danced
> And whenever I shouted my name
> I heard a silver echo roar in the wind.

The question posed is still difficult to resolve. After the fortunate Leadville silver bonanzas, followed by Horace's scandalous affair, divorce, and remarriage, the Tabor story faded into legend. In fact, the Tabors became legendary almost from the day of the discovery of the Little Pittsburg Mine in 1878. For contemporaries and those who came after, Horace, Augusta, and eventually Baby Doe represented the story of what mining might provide for fortunate individuals who tempted fate and won.

None of that story would have been obvious back in New England, where Augusta and Horace spent their childhoods. Nothing in their lives in those years seemed to point to anything exceptional ahead for either of them.

Born in Augusta, Maine, on March 29, 1833, Augusta Pierce grew up in the middle-class home of her building contractor and stonemason father. Augusta, the third daughter of her mother, Lucy, and father, William, was one of six sisters and three brothers. Poor health dogged Augusta until she reached her twenties, but her spirit and determination got her through these ailments. Augusta, the state's capital city, offered her a variety of cultural and educational opportunities unavailable to many rural New Englanders, and she matured into a refined young woman for that time in Maine. Indeed, her father and several neighbors held a liberal attitude toward the role of women. Augusta and her sisters grew up sure of their worth and able to move confidently in what remained primarily a man's world.

With terse New England reticence, she summarized her life before coming to Colorado in 1859: "I had lived in Kansas [for] two years. My native place is Maine. I married and came out to Kansas and we settled on a farm." There was much more to her and her life before the Pike's Peak gold rush than that.

HORACE HAD BEEN BORN (on November 26, 1830) and spent his youth in the isolated rural hamlet of Holland, in northern Vermont. Tabor and his two brothers and a sister grew up in this agricultural environment doing chores, working long hours on the farm, and receiving a public school education. Tabor later reminisced about those years, perhaps remembering more than actually happened!

> My parents were pretty strict in the way of discipline, reasonably so, still not so very strict, I don't think. We had a good common school education. At school I was always well near the head of the class. I have been very industrious all my life.
>
> Mathematics was as easy for me as it is for water to run down a hill. Geography was not so easy; grammar was easy for me. I never got far in algebra.

Like many young men, Horace became restless in his teenage years, particularly after his mother died and his father remarried a woman "who made it pretty hot around my ears." Holland offered little opportunity. As Tabor recalled, "There was not a respectable village in the whole township. It seemed to me as if there was no field for progress or advancement. I left at the age of nineteen. I resolved to try and hunt a better country to see what opportunities would be presented. I was a strong, robust boy; I have always had good health." Tabor then started on the trail that twenty-nine years later would place him in Leadville, Colorado.

After leaving home, Horace learned the stonecutter's trade, which in time carried him through Massachusetts to Augusta, Maine. There he worked for William Pierce and met and courted his daughter. Stonecutting and Maine did not match his expectations, even if Augusta did. He had a dream, a dream that could not be satisfied in New England or, for that matter, in the East.

The West of cheap land and opportunity beckoned him. To understand Horace and his life, that dream of a "promised land" of fortune and destiny must be kept in mind.

He went west alone to Lawrence, Kansas, arriving on a cold March morning in 1855. Those days in Kansas typified no ordinary westward movement of pioneers. Caught up in the increasingly volatile slavery issue between the North and South, Kansas became a testing field for the radicals of both camps. It was going to be either all slave or all free if they had their way. Horace had come in a party sent by the New England Emigrant Aid Company, which was determined to make Kansas free.

No radical in the free soil movement, Tabor moved to the central valley of the Kansas River and settled near the infant village of Zeandale, a few miles outside Manhattan. Here he took to farming, his early years on his father's farm standing him in good stead. By preemption, Horace secured 160 acres, and later, by borrowing the money, he purchased another 320 acres. Like the multitudes before him, he looked to farming in the West as the road to his dream.

Agriculture proved not to represent the royal road to wealth, however; farming in Kansas was hard and difficult in those early years. The land needed to be broken to the plow and weather conditions, and the growing season had to be understood and a home established.

Despite all this, Horace could not stand outside the slavery issue that gnawed at the very heart of Kansas and its future. He later said, "My politics were free soil. I have always been against slavery." Kansas split into two camps, exploding in 1855 and 1856. Tabor's growing interest in the cause appeared warm enough to secure his nomination and election to the Free Soil House of Representatives on a bitterly cold January election day. Each side was busy electing its own Kansas government.

Tabor went to the brief March meeting in the free soil capital of Topeka, then journeyed home to plow and plant his fields when the legislature adjourned on March 16, 1856. It reassembled on July 4. The House of Representatives met on the appointed day, only to have federal troops disperse the members. Tabor thought it a "great outrage" and blamed the disbanding on President Franklin Pierce, who he believed wanted Kansas to be a slave state. Farming seemed dull after that; nevertheless, Horace stayed with it, trying to turn his farm into a profitable venture.

He returned to Topeka for the January 1857 legislative session, although with Kansas calming down, this extralegal child of expediency was no longer needed. In later years he reflected with pleasure on the days when he stood against slavery. And in truth, it had taken courage to express one's views as a member of a legislature threatened by nearby enemies. What he had gained would prove valuable in the years ahead: necessary experience in parliamentary procedure and the art of frontier politics.

Tabor had other things on his mind that January. Horace was going back to Maine to marry Augusta. Having been engaged for the past two years, the couple was finally married on January 31, 1857. For nearly a month they remained in Augusta, Maine, then left for Kansas—a tiring, slow railroad trip, followed by a more pleasant boat ride up the Missouri River. For Augusta, that seemed the last pleasant moment for a while. She faced a shock when she first looked about her new prairie home. A small solitary cabin, which for the past two years had served as Horace's bachelor lodging, awaited her. All around it desolation, the prairie winds, and an entrapping loneliness dominated the scene. She had never envisioned the promised land this way. How different it appeared from her Maine home in late winter: "I sat down upon the trunk and cried; I had not been deceived in coming to this place. I knew perfectly well that the country was new, that there were no sawmills near, and no money in the territory. But I was homesick and could not conceal it from those about me."

Not one to fret interminably, August set about to work loyally with her husband in their search for fortune. Although small in frame, Augusta in the months and years ahead proved strong of heart and soul. Like so many other eastern women, she had the personality to adapt to the western frontier, and she did.

The Tabors had left New England for good, yet their roots there never left them. Both were industrious, dignified, and well educated. These roots colored them individually and affected their marital relationship and their reactions to their new homes and changing circumstances. Augusta was more hardworking and financially conservative, and Horace was more outgoing and free spending. In 1879, a quarter of a century after he came West, Horace was described as a Vermonter in "figure, speech, and temper of mind." Augusta remained the careful, modest New England woman who cautiously shepherded the family funds and planned thoroughly to have enough for their retirement years.

The next two years in Kansas showed the young married couple how slow a road to the promised land agriculture could be. To supplement their income, Horace turned again to work as a stonemason, and Augusta took in boarders and occasionally worked with her husband in the fields. Tabor later admitted that his Kansas days "offered me little inducement to remain there." Meanwhile, their only child, Maxey, was born, adding to their concerns. The prospects for the young family did not seem promising, despite their best efforts, when they, like thousands of other Americans, heard rumors of gold in Pike's Peak country in late summer of 1858.

GOLD PROMISED TO BE A FAST SHORTCUT TO FORTUNE. Nevertheless, Tabor had heard rumors before, almost the entire time he had been in Kansas, of gold farther to the west. This time, however, the rumors seemed more likely to be fact. Augusta and Horace weighed their options and decided in spring of 1859 to join thousands of their fellow Americans and rush to the new Pike's Peak goldfields. "I came out here for the purpose of mining, because we knew nothing of this country except as a mining country," Horace later commented. "I came for the express purpose of trying to make money enough out here to redeem that land [Kansas]."

In that wondrous spring of 1859, they and others rushed to the Pike's Peak country. It was a promised land more of rumor than of reality. As the first fifty-niners who arrived found out, little gold had actually been found, prices soared beyond the reach of many, and no one appeared to be getting rich. The "pilgrims" quickly returned home. Augusta recalled those days and their journey west. Her observations were as true for Leadville in 1878 as they were for Pike's Peak in 1859—the excitement, the expectations, the elation: "I never saw a country settled up with such greenhorns as Colorado. They were mostly from farms and some clerks. They were all young men from 18 to 30. I was there a good many years before we saw a man with gray hair. They thought they were going to have a second California; they gathered all the knowledge they could from books." Discouragingly, the Tabors continued to meet the "go-backers": "We met them every day and they advised us to go back." Undaunted, they pushed ahead. "We started with six months' provisions and thought if we did not find anything here we would go on to California," Augusta remembered. Fate intervened; they never went to California together.

They briefly camped in what was still rough-hewn Denver, then went into the mountains. Although Horace had come to mine, he knew he could not take Augusta and Maxey prospecting with him. So they camped near future Golden, near the mouth of Clear Creek Canyon, and Horace went on to the gold districts. The change from the Augusta Tabor of Kansas two years before to the Augusta of the Pike's Peak rush proved her mettle: "I stayed in camp and took care of the cattle and provisions. The cattle were footsore and could not go far, but I kept them from straying. I stayed there quite alone, there was no one there, no Indians, nothing there but just myself and our teams. Silence reigned around, not a soul but me and my baby, and I was a weakly woman." Augusta had been sick on the way out, but, undaunted, on she went. She had become a pioneering woman.

Horace traveled on to Payne's Bar, near where Idaho Springs would soon take hold, and came back to get his family. His wife recalled, "We were three weeks going from there to where Central is now. Had to make our road as we went. We could only make about three miles a day, a wagon had never been there before."

They struggled, finally, into Payne's Bar and got their first taste of Colorado mining camp life. They successfully teamed up— he prospecting and mining, she selling tasty baked goods to miners eager for home-cooked food. That combination, with a few variations, pulled the Tabors through the next eighteen years as they followed their will-o'-the-wisp dreams in the Colorado mountains. They made enough money that season to pay the debt on the Kansas farm; however, no thought existed of going home to Zeandale and back to Kansas farming. They planned to stay and find their fortune in the gold that beckoned just beyond their present location.

Initially, a setback occurred. An "old-timer" told Horace that a woman should not stay in the mountains in the winter, especially not with a small child. Although Tabor had found a promising claim, he heeded the warning, heading for Denver with his family. After finding them quarters, he went back, only to find his claim had been jumped. With the vague mining law of the day, Horace had no recourse, so he abandoned his claim. "There was no law in those days," Augusta sorrowfully noted.

They did not give up, however. With enough money to get through the winter, the Tabors waited for another spring and started for Colorado City, near Pike's Peak. Tabor thought he could get in on the ground floor of a town promotion, one "sure" way to make a profit if it panned out as planned. It did not.

Horace and Augusta heard new rumors of gold, west in the mountains along the Arkansas River. Off they went again. Such was the lure of gold, for certainly Horace, and probably Augusta as well, had caught gold fever. Gold or silver fever can long lie dormant, but once caught, it flares time and time again, regardless of one's age or experience. Hope triumphed over reality in nineteenth-century Colorado or Nevada or anywhere in the mining West.

Eventually, after another slow and troublesome journey, the Tabors reached California Gulch, the site of a new "bonanza." This time they succeeded in being one of the fortunate first arrivals, and Tabor hurriedly went in search of a claim. They did not know it, but California Gulch, the 1860 placer "poor man's bonanza," swung along on the south edge of the future site of Leadville. For the first time, although not the last, the Tabors found prosperity in that district.

Augusta's "Mr. Tabor" found a rich claim, washing out $5,000–$7,000 that summer, and the men in the gulch honored her as the first woman to arrive by building the Tabors a log cabin in two days. Perhaps they did it with malicious aforethought, as well as to honor her pioneering spirit. Augusta related, "There were so many men who could not cook and did not like men's cooking and would insist upon boarding where there was a woman and they would board there all they could." She took in boarders that summer and became, in an informal manner, the postmistress of her portion of the gulch, or Oro City, as the cabins strung along California Gulch were finally called.

The days passed swiftly, the green of summer fading to the aspen yellow of fall. Oro City, too, faded from the wonder of the spring to a tired district before the snows came. By that time Augusta and Maxey had gone back to Maine for a visit, the first reward of their new wealth. Relying on his Kansas experience, Horace dabbled in the creation of a new territory they wanted to call Jefferson. He was elected to the legislature again, although it proved no more lasting than his Kansas experience. Congress would not recognize their handiwork and eventually created Colorado Territory in February 1861.

In spring 1861 the reunited Tabors made an important decision. Having observed the profits made by shrewd businessmen, they discussed the possibility of opening a store. They did so, with Augusta serving as manager and postmistress. Horace continued his mining, with small success.

THE TRANSITORY LIFE OF THE MINING WEST was no better shown than at Oro City that summer, as people moved in and out, confronted with "dull times" and "general gloom." In contrast, just to the northeast, across the Mosquito Range, glimmered the new promised land. As soon as winter let go its grip, the rush started, in June 1861, to Lauret City, better known as Buckskin Joe—a camp "with a bright and promising future."

Augusta and Horace faced a choice—they could stay in declining California Gulch or follow the golden goddess to another newly proclaimed bonanza. They decided to move. Gold fever carried the day. They packed furniture, supplies, and merchandise and migrated. No longer poor—they would never be again—they now resided in the respectable upper class of mining camp society, merchants, and mining folk.

For the next seven years they stayed at Buckskin Joe. The Tabor store, with the important post office designation, bedrocked the family while Horace wheeled and dealt with mines, less as a miner now than as an owner and operator. For a while, their new home offered better prospects than Oro City had. "The liveliest little burg" in the southern mines was promoted as the "most extensive and probably richest mining country in the Territory."

Augusta was pleased when a visitor proclaimed that Buckskin Joe had "more respectable families, nice[r] folks" than any other mountain town except "Nevadaville and Central City." Sadly, these days did not last. Within a couple of seasons, Buckskin Joe, too, slipped into decline. This time the Tabors stayed, living in the back of their general store.

Horace had less success with his mining ventures but more with his store than had been the case at Oro City. Gaining a reputation as a "miners' sutler," he was willing to assist poor prospectors when they needed help. He would grubstake scores of them over the years. The Tabors resided there while the Civil War waged back in the states. They were there when Radical Republicans tried to impeach President Andrew Johnson and as construction of the transcontinental railroad started from the east and the west. They also stayed as Colorado's overall mining fortunes slid into nearly a decade-long spell of gloom and despair. Lack of working capital, poor transportation, the high cost of living, problems of underground mining, and difficult ore to mill (plus a terrible reputation gained from an 1863–1864 frenzy of mining speculation) left Colorado a pariah among western mining regions.

Buckskin Joe mirrored what was happening throughout the territory. Still, a few honors came Horace's way. Although never one of the "boys in blue," he was a fifty-niner, a distinction he held with honor throughout his life. As early as 1866 he was elected vice president of the Pioneer Association of Park County. For a short time Horace also served as superintendent of schools in the county.

Their days at Buckskin Joe provide the best pre-Leadville glimpse of these two fascinating individuals and their home life. Mail carrier Samuel Leach wrote several letters in 1862 and 1863 in which he talked about his friends the Tabors. His shrewd and perceptive insights bring Augusta and Horace to life.

For example, in an October 1862 letter, he described that "they are considered well to do here and they certainly are thrifty like down eastern Yankees." Of Augusta he said, "She is a good cook and the men like her pretty well although she is a driver." After helping her sort out the mail, the three of them would "play seven-up and high-five for a while and she often takes a hand."

A March 10, 1863, letter caught the essence of the two as few other documents have. Leach had visited the Tabors on a Sunday afternoon. He again described his friends' present circumstances and added what they planned for their future: "The Tabors are naturally thrifty, she more so perhaps than he is. In addition to tending store and looking after the mail she keeps boarders and makes a profit at it. They have accumulated almost twenty thousand dollars in the time they have been in this territory and are planning to make a fortune here and return to New England to enjoy it in their old age."

Apparently, the Tabors had been discussing that future, and Sam happened to step into the middle of a disagreement. Horace mentioned his dreams to him: "Sam, twenty years from now I shall have enough money to take things easy three months in each year and live comfortably at hotels in New York or Washington." That was too much for Augusta, who expressed what must have been some pent-up emotions and frustrations from living with her husband, far from the comforts of her former New England home. Augusta had a temper; one person described her as "violently tempered." Leach continued:

> His wife spoke up and said that she had no such thought but that they both ought to work and save as long as they were able to do so to make sure that they would be provided for in the lean years when they reached old age. She said he liked his leisure too well and did not exert himself as fully as he might do but took too much time off as it was for fishing, hunting and playing cards. She said he was too easy and if it were not for her looking out for him they would not have a dollar in the world.

The Tabors argued over retirement and related matters. Sam Leach wisely "kept my mouth shut." He concluded, "I like them both very much, each of them has fine qualities and they are good company."

A couple of months later another letter gave more insight into Horace and perhaps hinted at the truth of some of his wife's accusations. Tabor, on his way to go fishing, dropped by Sam's cabin to give him a pot of beans Augusta had made: "I asked Mr. Tabor what he expected to catch as it was early for trout in the streams about here, and he said nothing at all—he was going for the sake of going fishing, and laughed and went off in his lumbering fashion, pitching along in his high boots." Sam continued, "He is very good-natured and full of fun and he has to take days off every now and then."

Another contemporary miner, Nathan Hurd, later called Augusta "an angel of mercy" whose infinite kindness of heart and acts of benevolence were legion. Tabor, too, he thought, had a kind heart and was a much better man than he was later "accredited" to be.

Augusta reinforced that image of her role during the mining days before the Leadville bonanza. Interviewed in 1884, she described those earlier times: "Really, the women did more in the early days than the men. There was so much for them to do, the sick to take care of. I have had so many unfortunate men shot by accident brought to my cabin to take care of." She also recalled a discussion about Maxey's future. Horace wanted him to work in the store, and Augusta favored his going to school: "I told him I would go into the store and do all the boy could do. I went into the store, and he found I was a better hand at keeping the books than he was."

These insights paint an engrossing portrait of the two before they became millionaires. They appear in many ways much as they later would, with a good reputation as individuals and as neighbors, gained over a decade on the Colorado frontier. Both were hardworking, but differences in temperament and lifestyle had obviously already surfaced in the Tabor family. At the moment, they did not seem serious.

By winter of 1867–1868, the Tabors had to make another choice. Buckskin Joe had seen better days and did not promise much of a future. The depressed Colorado mining situation offered few opportunities. They might go to Georgetown, where silver mining beckoned, although no really promising new districts appeared to be opening. They decided to leave and return back across the Mosquito Range to California Gulch and Oro City. This was not the placer Oro City but a hard-rock hamlet that had migrated up near the headwaters of the gulch where the mines were located.

In late spring of 1868, when the passes opened, the Tabors moved yet another time. They would stay in Oro City until 1877. The familiar pattern resumed: the store opened, miners were grubstaked, and Horace became postmaster and express agent. Oro City, though, languished in the backwater of Colorado mining. Seemingly, these two fifty-niners, who had been following their golden dreams for nearly twenty years, had taken a step backward.

The Tabors were Oro City's outstanding merchants, not necessarily a claim to fame or prosperity. A Denver merchant remarked, "He [Horace Tabor] is an honest man and will pay his bills when he can, but what business can he do in Lake County? There isn't enough business there to keep a cat alive." An R. G. Dun reporter sent this review of Tabor to the company: "Oro City, December 27, 1876. Is a very shrewd businessman and not liable to lose money, has a good chance to make money as he has no competition. Estimated worth say $15,000."

That was Horace Tabor the businessman. The Tabors had reached middle age and, although easily maintaining themselves, had not found their promised land.

Continuing his dabbling in politics, Horace was elected county treasurer in 1876. He got caught up in a nasty political squabble that same year involving his supposed cruelty to Augusta and her elopement with another man. That accusation was blatantly false and came to nothing. If he had not known it before, Horace found out that Colorado politics could be rough!

Horace Tabor the mining man worked as hard as the businessman. He promoted his district and his county whenever he could. As early as June 1868, the *Rocky Mountain News* reported he had come down to Denver with "some very rich" gold quartz samples plus 50 ounces of placer gold. He continued grubstaking with its low batting average, accepting his misfortunes without complaining. Augusta apparently did not accept these failed grubstakes. She fretted. Tabor again studied hard-rock mining and understood the problems that confronted his district—isolation, poor transportation, lack of capital, and low-grade ore bodies.

Horace also knew silver had been found nearby. In fact, he dabbled in silver and gold claims and had silver ore assayed at the local assay office. By 1876, mining people generally recognized that silver existed in the California Gulch region. The only question remaining—how rich—was about to be answered in bonanza terms. In the winter-freed late spring of 1877, prospecting started early.

Augusta and Horace again became caught up in a mining rush, this one in their backyard.

THAT SPRING REKINDLED ONCE MORE FOR THE TABORS the excitement of 1859, 1860, 1861, and 1868—the intoxication of a mining rush, with all the long-deferred dreams of wealth. Horace correctly gauged that Oro would not be the camp of the future. They packed up and moved slightly over 2½ miles down the gulch and a little northward to an as-yet-unnamed infant camp. This move, so short a distance in mileage, represented a lifetime in its implications.

The Tabors arrived in July, the second merchants on the scene. Postmaster Tabor also appeared in the store. One still had to be cautious and cover all business bets, and customers buying groceries after getting their mail proved as advantageous as ever. From the day he arrived, the "old man," as they often called him (forty-six was old for a mining rush), settled into an easy routine as one of the camp's leading citizens and important merchants. The H.A.W. Tabor general provisions and outfitting store stood on Chestnut Street, the camp's leading business street. The next January, Horace and four others were appointed commissioners and election judge to "perfect a town organization." They drafted the incorporation papers, held an election in February, and Mayor

Tabor assumed office. He was given credit for suggesting the name Leadville, although others also claimed that honor.

It mattered little. Augusta and Horace were on the ground floor of the greatest rush and boom they had ever experienced. The mayor found himself busy with a host of matters that needed to be resolved in the rapidly changing conditions of Leadville. Ordinances had to be passed, officials selected for offices (and often quickly replaced as they rushed hither and yon), a municipal water source found and developed, fire prevented, and the poor helped. Many people rushed into a boom with too many dreams and too few resources.

Tabor had never seen such problems or the magnitude of business in his career as postmaster in smaller mining camps. Because the government bureaucracy ground slowly, Leadville was rated a fourth-class post office long after it became a bustling mining town. The postmaster's salary was based on the sale of stamps. Horace ran the post office out of his own pocket, hiring an increasingly larger staff to handle the mail swamping the clerks.

What was Leadville during those days? Visitors called it "roaring," "the Magic City," a "fast place," a "glorious camp," and a "marvel." Author/writer Mary Hallock Foote, on her way to join her mining husband, simply said, "All roads lead to Leadville." The camp became a town in the twinkling of an eye and had nearly 15,000 people by the census count in 1880. The second-largest community in Colorado had emerged as an instant city. "The father of Leadville" watched over his town with pride.

Mining, though, never left Tabor's mind. He continued to grubstake prospectors, as he had for years. In return for what supplies he provided them, they promised him a share of whatever they found. So far, that had added little to the Tabor coffers. Then, on or about April 20, 1878, Tabor's fortune changed.

TWO NONDESCRIPT PROSPECTORS CAME INTO HIS STORE asking for a grubstake; Tabor was to receive one-third of anything they discovered. George Hook and August Rische displayed little experience with Leadville ores, or much else for that matter. Tabor tried his luck one more time. Rische and Hook walked out of Tabor's store and tramped up onto Fryer Hill into legend. Here, where George Fryer had found the New Discovery Mine, they discovered the richest bonanza in the area. The story at this point becomes confused. The sequence must have gone like this: they found a likely-looking spot that appeared promising and staked a claim.

By coincidence (some would call it luck), Hook and Rische picked the one spot on Fryer Hill where the mineral came closest to the surface. After digging down 26 or 27 feet, they hit a vein of extremely rich silver carbonate ore on May 1. Two of the most unlikely prospectors Tabor had ever grubstaked had discovered the Little Pittsburg Mine, one of Leadville's and the Rocky Mountains' greatest mines.

From that time on, Tabor's fortune and fame took wing. The story became well-known, reaching legendary status within months. When he purchased the Chrysolite Mine and opened it into a second bonanza, then followed in 1879 with the Matchless, the third of his opulent mines, it seemed Tabor could make no mining errors. Tabor had purchased the last one, as he said, for "pin money," but he turned it into a bonanza. The Matchless would become the most immortal of Tabor's mines. His income soared to thousands of dollars per week.

The press could not let such a good story go to waste. Leadville and its mines were front-page news, and to the public Tabor symbolized Leadville. Tabor, after all, represented the bountiful blessing mining could bestow on an individual. This fifty-niner had stuck it out; most of his contemporaries had long ago gone home or drifted on to other mining territories. Horace at last had found his promised land. The fact that silver, not gold, had made the Tabors millionaires mattered little. Journalists had a field day with the "rags to riches" story of a poor Vermont stonemason who had stumbled on a fortune in the Colorado mountains. A Michigan paper claimed Tabor as a former citizen, now worth $50 million, who at the time he struck carbonates was working for day wages as a stonecutter!

The legend grew with each passing year. The Tabors, even without any further developments, had come to embody mining as no one else of their Colorado generation would.

Horace Tabor. Courtesy, Library of Congress

Unfortunately, wealth did not bring happiness. Tabor was busy with his now varied investments. He sold the mercantile store, opened a bank, helped bring gas lighting and the telephone to the town, built the Tabor Opera House (Leadville's "most beautiful brick structure"), and moved Augusta into a new frame home off Harrison Avenue. Their old homesite had been the spot where the opera house now glistened. "I never knew a man as busy as I was in Leadville at that time," he later mentioned. And he was right. Augusta, however, increasingly slipped away and was not part of his expanding world.

Horace thoroughly enjoyed their wealth and prestige, but fame and fortune did not sit well with Augusta. She remained the rock-ribbed New England woman appalled by the extravagances suddenly within their reach and the social circle they now entered. This industrious, pioneering woman, who enjoyed housework and gardening, seemed out of place. If Horace ever stopped to consider his wife's feelings in these matters, he quickly put such thoughts aside.

Tabor quickly entered politics with his old enthusiasm, bankrolling the Republican Party in election after election. Nominated for lieutenant governor in 1878, he won the two-year term and then served another when the winning GOP candidate in 1880 was killed before taking office. Augusta and Tabor moved to bustling Denver, a town that had changed greatly since they had first seen it twenty years ago. Leadville silver was just beginning to arrive in the city, which would alter Denver more in the next ten years than it had in the previous two decades.

Leadville's silver millionaire became a big part of that impact and transformation. He built the five-story Tabor Block that dominated the posh Larimer Street business district. "A noble monument of enterprise, faith and pluck," wrote a captivated reporter. Tabor had more in mind. He purchased land on the corner of Sixteenth and Curtis and set in motion his plans to build an opera house—not any opera house but the Tabor Grand Opera. The $850,000 masterpiece opened the evening of September 5, 1881, with a performance by the renowned Emma Abbott Company.

That evening proved the apex of Tabor's fame. Called to the stage amid "vociferous applause," Horace stood while his career was briefly reviewed. He was presented with an autograph album and a gold watch fob, symbolizing his rise from miner to owner

Augusta Tabor. Courtesy, Colorado Historical Society

of the Tabor Grand. It was done in "appreciation for the love which you have bestowed upon Denver and her people." In modest reply, Horace called Denver, with a bit of understandable chauvinism, the "finest city on the American continent": "I said if Denver is to have an opera house it should be worthy of the city. Here is the opera house, I shall leave it to your judgment if I have done my duty in this respect [applause]. Here is this beautiful album

Elizabeth "Baby Doe" Tabor. Courtesy, Colorado Historical Society

and fob chain—as beautiful as can be. I shall prize them every hour I live. I shall prize them not for their price value but for the spirit in which they are given."

"PERFECTION!" headlined one *Rocky Mountain News* article. "It will remain a monument to Denver enterprise for many years to come and a monument of which anyone might be proud." Eugene Field, *Denver Tribune* editor and poet, who had enjoyed immense fun at Tabor's expense in the pages of his newspaper, rose to the occasion.

> The opera House—a union grand
>   Of capital and labor—
> Long will the stately structure stand
>   A monument to Tabor!

Only Tabor enjoyed the evening. Augusta did not attend. The Tabor box sat hauntingly empty. Augusta had not wanted it that way. She pleaded with her husband in a poignant letter: "Believe me that none will be more proud of it than your *broken hearted wife*. Will you not take me there and by so doing stop the gossip that is busy with *our* affairs?" He would not; instead, a heavily veiled woman shared his thoughts and the opera house that night.

Their wealth and different attitudes toward it had inflamed the marital troubles seen back at Buckskin Joe. They had separated, no doubt, at least in part because of Horace's well-rumored wanderings from his marriage bed with, as Augusta called them, "lewd women." Despite Augusta's wishes, there would be no reconciliation. On January 1, 1883, the brokenhearted Augusta sadly commented that the divorce had not been "willingly asked for." On the last day of the month, their twenty-sixth wedding anniversary, she made one last effort. She pleaded with Horace: "Now you have had the honors of senatorship which you deserted me for. And when your month is [up] come home and let us live in harmony. As I will come to you." She would not have the chance to carry out her forlorn attempt at reconciliation.

Horace's divorce came in the midst of his campaign for the U.S. Senate. Although he did not win the seat, Tabor received the "consolation prize" of the remaining thirty days of Henry Teller's term. Teller's appointment as secretary of the interior in President Chester Arthur's cabinet had opened the senatorship. Although it was not for a full term, Tabor had achieved the highest elective office in Colorado in the nineteenth century. At least he and other mining men, who repeatedly vied for the position, thought so.

Tabor ended his thirty-day term with a "sensation," his lavishly staged remarriage to Elizabeth McCourt Doe, with President Chester Arthur, Secretary Teller, Colorado's congressional delegation, and others in attendance. The love-struck senator, age fifty-two, married a twenty-eight-year-old petite, vivacious grass widow whom he had met in Leadville several years before.

BORN IN OSHKOSH, WISCONSIN, Elizabeth grew up there and married Harvey Doe, son of a prominent family. Even at a young age she had a hometown reputation for showing both a taste for masculine flattery and a trace of exhibitionism in flaunting her beauty and figure. Belying this image was the fact, as the opera states, that she "had a head on her shoulders." She would demonstrate that repeatedly throughout her life. Like so many others, the Does moved west in the late 1870s to seek their fortune—to Central City to manage Harvey's father's mining property there.

The Fourth of July Mine did not "pan out," as the mining saying went. The Does found themselves in a mining and district town that had slipped past its prime and was not like what his father had seen when he lived there in the early 1860s. Expenses outran income, and to help curb costs Elizabeth apparently worked underground beside Harvey, almost unheard of for a woman in that era. Mining was a man's world, but Elizabeth proved no ordinary Victorian lady. Both Harvey and the mines failed Lizzie, and she divorced him in 1880. In Central City, meanwhile, she gained the nickname "Baby Doe" and attained local fame as one of Colorado's most attractive women. Other men entered her life, and the free-spirited Baby Doe flaunted Victorian sensibilities. Women did not like Lizzie even before the Tabor uproar.

She left declining Central and its opera house to move to booming Leadville. After the divorce her activities are somewhat clouded, but she picked *the* Colorado mining town in which to stake her future. Lizzie and Leadville were a perfect match. Leadville also proudly embraced a free-spirited, tolerant reputation, as well as "buckets galore of silver ore," and reveled in its wide-open notoriety. At its apex of silver wealth, power, and fame, the town offered a bonanza of opportunities to those willing to gamble on tomorrow. Baby Doe had caught up with her destiny.

How she and Horace met, what happened, and why are lost to history. Regardless, Horace fell head over heels in love. Their affair had pushed the infatuated suitor to pressure Augusta for a divorce.

Back in Colorado, tongues wagged, gossip multiplied, and the Tabors found themselves in a difficult situation when William Bush, Horace's right-hand man, had a falling-out with his employer. The dispute ended in the courts, and the dirty linen was dragged through the press. The affair proved bad enough but was compounded by a fraudulent Durango divorce and a secret St. Louis marriage in September 1882. Tabor had been a bigamist and perjured himself when signing on the marriage application "that we are both single and unmarried." The whys of this series of events are also lost to history. Perhaps Baby Doe found herself in a family way, and Tabor wanted to legitimize the affair. If so, she lost the baby. Other facts about the Augusta and Horace hassle over a divorce in 1882 came out, including their wealth and marital problems.

Tabor, with his remarriage and the newsy trial, had crossed his personal Rubicon. No longer would he be considered "fit" as a political candidate, and the Tabors would no longer be welcomed by Denver society. Maybe it mattered little to him and Baby Doe. They were happily married, much in love, and the parents—by the end of the decade—of two young daughters, Elizabeth and Rose Mary. They also had a son, who died at birth.

Tabor believed it only took one Little Pittsburg or Matchless to redeem a score or more of poor investments, lavishly spreading his money around Colorado. He became the first Colorado mining millionaire to reinvest his fortune at home, and he did so with faith in the future and himself. That faith alone constitutes his greatest Colorado significance. Unfortunately, with the plunging price of silver, his mines decreased production, and when he failed to hit another bonanza, his fortune declined. Good money went after bad, and even his nonmining investments could not sustain him.

By the 1890s Horace was "mortgaged to the hilt" and desperately trying to find a way out of his economic morass. That was when the silver issue became so prominent in his life. The price of silver had been falling steadily since the mid-1870s, even with attempts by the federal government to stabilize the situation. Silver had dropped from $1.35 an ounce to the 90-cents-an-ounce range against the rising cost of mining as miners dug deeper into the earth. Coloradans and other silver producers throughout the Rocky Mountains blamed the decline on a conspiracy of eastern and foreign bankers, investors, businessmen, and moneylenders, aided and abetted by the conservative, business-oriented Republican Party. Plots and guilty parties made for good reading but little else. The real cause was the overproduction of the silver mines against the declining international use of silver for coinage and the stagnant industrial and jewelry markets.

The cry of "Free Silver" and "Sixteen to One" (making 16 ounces of silver equal to 1 ounce of gold, thereby raising the price of the former to $1.25) swept Colorado and the silver-producing states. Neither the Democrats nor the Republicans responded, so a new party did—the People's, or Populist, Party. After years of loyalty to the Republican Party, Horace and many others left the Grand Old Party. Tabor had long been a leading spokesman in the silver cause, and while his finances still allowed it, he helped bankroll the Populists in the state. They did very well in the 1890s in Colorado and some other western states for a new third party.

The climax came in the 1896 presidential election, when the Democrats nominated William Jennings Bryan and adopted Free Silver and almost the entire Populist platform. The Republicans selected William McKinley and gold. The lines were clearly drawn, and Coloradans voted overwhelmingly (85 percent) for the silver-tongued orator. Alas, he lost nationally. Free Silver was dead. The silver mines would not be rescued by that hope.

Regardless of whether a higher price for silver would have saved it, Tabor's empire was problematic. He was heavily mortgaged and deeply in debt, so the harsh crash of 1893 and the subsequent devastating depression pushed him beyond his limits.

It was the worst depression in Colorado's history and lasted the better part of the decade. Tabor could not ride out the storm because he had no major producing mines left to fall back on. One by one, he lost all his possessions. Stubbornly, Horace never declared bankruptcy and, as best he could, tried to pay his debts.

Fortunately, political friends came to the rescue. Horace was appointed postmaster of Denver, and he, Baby Doe, and the two girls could move into rooms in the Windsor Hotel. He had come around almost to where he had started a long generation ago. Those unforgettable words of the English poet Charles Kingsley, which Horace had placed on the drop curtain of the Tabor Grand Theater, now seemed prophetic: "So fleet the works of men back to the earth again; Ancient and holy things fade like a dream."

Once again Horace had rebounded from adversity and watched a changing America, a world power now, as it won the Spanish American War and gained an empire. By 1899 some of the bounce had returned to his step. The world around him appeared drastically different from when the fifty-niner had arrived at Payne's Bar. A Civil War had been fought, and modern, industrial/urban America had emerged. Now he and his generation had become relics of another age, as Coloradans prepared to enter a new century. Even his mining world only lived on in a few places in Colorado and the West. Americans were still interested in those old things, but for them the new world of the automobile, movies, phonographs, and electrical gadgets held more promise. They were ready to move on.

Tabor would not go with them. He died from peritonitis on April 10, 1899. The quest of Horace Austin Warner Tabor ended; the legend lived on.

"How can a man measure himself?" He had helped make Kansas a "free land for free people." Tabor journeyed to the Rocky Mountains as part of one of the most celebrated sagas of the nineteenth century, the Pike's Peak gold rush, a fifty-niner miner. Colorado mining man; the patron of Leadville, Denver, and Colorado; the energetic businessman; the investor with faith in Colorado's future; the politician and defender of the true creed "silver"; the husband and father—Horace lived all these roles to the fullest.

The *Denver Post,* in its April 10, 1899, eulogy, captured the heart of Tabor's contribution: he "loved Colorado and Denver."

Horace had come west as a pioneer, to a land unsettled and untamed. Now a definable frontier no longer existed. Colorado had not even been a name on the map in 1859; now it was a state with a population of over 500,000. Denver had been little but a struggling, jerry-built village along the South Platte; now it had earned the title "Queen of the Mountains and Plains." In his own way, however large or small, Horace Tabor had helped bring this about. What regrets he might have felt were minor compared with the sweep of change since he first came west to Kansas and Colorado.

THE BALLAD OF
BABY DOE
John Moriarty, Conductor
Central City, 1981, 1988, 1996

T HE STORY OF B ABY D OE and also the opera written
about her have fascinated me for years. I started collecting
Tabor and Baby Doe books years ago, after my first brush
with the opera in 1961 when we performed it at the Santa Fe
Opera.

Writing for the operatic stage is a little different from writing a
play or a novel. If the opera has a basis in historical fact, sometimes the facts have to be adjusted to accommodate the limita-
tions and demands of the theater. History is seldom tidy. Time
spans often must be compressed, motivations need to be clarified
(and sometimes simplified), and the advantages and shortcomings of the singing voice have to be considered. Douglas Moore
and John Latouche took what they needed from history, and the

adjustments they made are, in actuality, very minor. They managed to telescope into a very condensed time frame the events of the fifty-five-year span.

We usually consider that this opera has three main characters. Actually, there are four: Baby Doe, Augusta, Horace, and the Matchless Mine. The first scene opens with a drunken miner saying that Tabor wants to buy his Matchless Mine. The Matchless Mine is introduced even before Tabor, Baby, or Augusta. It begins the opera, and it ends the opera.

In that first scene we learn that Tabor wants to buy the mine. Later, in Scene 3, Augusta finds Horace's check made out to Jack Sands for purchase of the mine. References to the mine abound in Act II, with two of the five scenes set in that location. And finally, Baby Doe sings her last piece at the mine while the snow begins to fall around her.

THE STYLE EMPLOYED BY DOUGLAS MOORE FOR THIS OPERA is very simple and very moving. It is folksy, unpretentious, and nostalgic. Throughout the opera it provides a wonderful feeling of time and place. As all great theater composers have done, the music he provides for his characters is as revealing as the words they sing. Baby's music is warm, sentimental, sometimes banal, often touching in its simplicity. Horace's music undergoes a development that matches the development of the character, beginning with the bluster and braggadocio of the opening scene and proceeding to the agonized introspection of his final scene. For Augusta, Moore writes music in Act I that is very angular, thorny, unbending; in Act II, the angularity is gradually softened until it finally yields to the inner anguish of her great monologue. This is masterful character writing. The musical language should not be dismissed lightly merely because it sounds naive and simplistic at first hearing. It is not as simple as it sounds, as a detailed musical analysis (not the scope of this chapter) would show. Rather, it is a cleverly crafted sleight of pen intended to create the illusion of a nineteenth-century context.

It may well be that Moore took his cue from John Latouche, whose text is peppered with old-fashioned expressions calculated to reveal character and to evoke a certain period. Here, too, each character has his or her own style of language. Baby's lines could never be mistaken for Augusta's, for example. Certainly, Latouche provided Moore with a magnificent framework for the score. The first act builds logically, through contrasting scenes, to the brightness and joy of the wedding scene—a brightness dimmed only temporarily by revelations of divorce and then rescued by the arrival of President Arthur.

ACT II PROGRESSES INEXORABLY through scenes of emotional and financial disintegration to the final scene when Horace, now a defeated man, has nothing left but his memories and his cherished Baby Doe. The Aristotelian plan of the libretto is fulfilled, as Baby finds her redemption through her refusal to let go of her love for Horace, keeping it alive during her long vigil at the Matchless Mine.

It must be accepted that Baby Doe deliberately goes after Horace for the wealth and position he represents. A commonplace operatic love-at-first-sight situation would not have been worthy of John Latouche, nor would it have led to any kind of interesting development. On the other hand, a relationship that begins as a rather tawdry affair and that turns into something quite different is entirely stage worthy. In the fourth scene of Act I, Baby admits (in a letter to her mother) that her first motives in seeking out Horace were reprehensible, that she was looking for "a man so rich and powerful that he could give me anything and make me like a princess." This admission causes us to think back to Scene 2 of the same act. Was the "Willow Song" intended to attract Horace's attention? If Baby has overheard the conversation of the saloon girls, Kate and Meg, and if she has noticed Horace's reaction to it, then the case seems likely. In any event, their first extended conversation, after the "Willow Song," is laced with extravagant compliments that each bestows on the other. A mutual seduction is taking place, interrupted by the soon-to-be-wronged wife calling Horace to bed.

In the early part of Act I, Scene 3, we learn that Horace is going ahead with his plans to buy the Matchless Mine, that Augusta resents being left out of his business dealings, that she craves attention from Horace, and, finally, that the affair she has suspected does indeed exist. We also learn that she is a fighter and intends to do whatever she can to keep her husband.

IN THE FOLLOWING SCENE IN THE LOBBY of the Clarendon Hotel, Baby has her crisis of conscience and has decided that an affair with a married man, no matter how wealthy, is not exactly what her mother had in mind. This is all set forth in that most dependable of operatic devices: a letter that is read (sung) aloud. In the course of the confrontation scene that follows, Augusta inadvertently convinces Baby to stay. In a speech that reveals more about herself than about Horace, she describes him as a person ("the man is a child") who is immature, weak, easily led around, and needing her control. Baby decides that Augusta does not understand this man and does not recognize his positive qualities. In time, Baby will come to know and accept his shortcomings and will then develop a relationship in which he is "husband, father, child" to her. The historical Baby Doe was known as a charmer, a woman who knew how to handle men and make them feel wonderful. This quality is stressed throughout the opera, nowhere more tellingly than in the wedding reception scene.

In the course of the party, an argument has developed between Horace and four State Department bureaucrats on the subject of gold coinage versus silver. Baby steps into the fray and handles both sides with consummate diplomacy, allowing that gold has its good points, but her preference is for silver because it has so many pleasant and romantic connotations for her. Underlying the rather sugary text is the concept that Baby identifies silver with Horace, and that idea continues to be developed in Act II.

The occasion is a party at the Windsor Hotel in Denver, where Horace is being honored. A surprise visit is made by Augusta, who advises Baby that silver is about to crash and that Horace will thereby lose his wealth. Horace believes that silver's problems are temporary and begs Baby to stand by him. She enthusiastically agrees, singing "Place my bet on silver," meaning, of course, "Place my bet on Horace." Augusta has advised Baby to sell the

Matchless Mine. Horace now extracts a promise from Baby that she will hold on to the Matchless no matter what happens. By pledging allegiance to the Matchless, Baby pledges her allegiance to Horace.

THE MATCHLESS MINE IS THE SCENE of a political rally attended by William Jennings Bryan, the Democratic candidate in 1896, running on a Free Silver platform. Horace's former cronies have deserted him, as they have seen his fortunes wane. Baby, of course, has remained steadfast, and now Horace, silver, and the Matchless begin to intertwine. The optimistic marching song at the end of the scene turns sour as newsboys cry out the devastating headlines that McKinley has won the election. Bryan's defeat is Horace's defeat. Now, at age sixty-six, he knows he is too old to rebuild his fortune.

The scene that follows is an imagined meeting between Augusta and Baby's mother. Mrs. McCourt pleads for help from Augusta, now a wealthy woman, but a calcified pride prevents her from giving any assistance. A powerful monologue follows in which we are allowed to peer into the heart of Augusta Tabor. She still loves Horace, in spite of his rejection of her, but she dwells in the past and cannot forgive him.

This intense and emotional scene is followed by the great final scene of the opera. Horace, old and broken, has returned to the scene of one of his greatest triumphs: his monument to himself, the Tabor Grand Opera House in Denver. Alone on the stage, his life passes before his eyes as ghosts reenact his moments of success and list his achievements. The crescendo of triumphs culminates in a grand chorus celebrating the opening of this very building.

BUT THE EXHILARATION OF THAT MOMENT dissipates quickly into self-doubts and recriminations. "How can a man measure himself," he asks. He wanted to build great buildings and do great things, but perhaps it will all fade. Augusta is still rattling around in his mind. Her ghost reminds him of his failure and predicts worse to come. Earlier in the same scene, there is a confusion between Augusta and Tabor's mother who, it is implied, also regarded him as a failure—even as a boy. Augusta's ghost gives him a glimpse into the future: one daughter will run away and deny the Tabor name; another will end her life as an alcoholic drug addict and prostitute. A desperate passage, punctuated by erratic heartbeats in the tympani, is followed by Tabor's collapse and the entrance of Baby Doe, who has come to find him. He dies in her arms, and as she sings her final aria, the passage of thirty-six years is implied. She now stands faithfully by the Matchless Mine because Horace, silver, and the mine have all become one for her. As the snow begins to fall, she declares her love to be unchanging for the man who was "husband, father, child."

The Revisions

During the premiere performance of *The Ballad of Baby Doe* at Central City in 1956, Moore and Latouche decided that a number of revisions were in order. Foremost of these was the inclusion of a whole new scene, the scene set in a Denver men's club in Act II. It was felt that a bridge was needed between the Windsor Hotel scene (Tabor at his peak) and the political rally at the Matchless Mine (Tabor impoverished but still optimistic). The so-called poker scene would outline the decline of Horace's fortunes and indicate a growing desperation on his part. The new scene accomplished the bridge masterfully, with Moore insinuating some of the political rally music into the scene and adding a splendid monologue for Tabor at the end.

One of the first cuts to be made was in the opening scene of Act I. Between the opening bars of the orchestral introduction and the pistol shot, there was originally a lengthy passage of local color, with saloon girls and miners cavorting in front of the Tabor Opera House. The passage added little and held up the beginning of the real action. Plenty of local color remains in the chorus of miners and the ensuing square dance, and the opening scene gains much in conciseness.

AUDIENCES IN CENTRAL CITY THAT SUMMER heard two arias that were replaced before subsequent productions. The infamous "Wake, snakes" aria, which Baby originally sang in the first scene of Act II and which made her seem unflatteringly vindictive, was replaced by the tamer and more conventional "The fine ladies walk."

The big surprise in this department is that the 1956 audiences were denied the pleasure of hearing Horace's aria "Warm as the autumn light." It was written as a substitution for "Out of the darkness," a short piece that has little to commend it.

The rest of the revisions were minor: some ethnic references were deleted in Act I; some unnecessary (and annoying) ornithological references were done away with; and an uninspired children's game was removed from the Bryan scene.

John Latouche had finished the text revisions, both new arias, and the poker scene when he was found dead from a heart attack on August 7, 1956. That was one month to the day after the premiere of *The Ballad of Baby Doe*.

Historical Adjustments

Latouche and Moore made surprisingly few historical adjustments. The greatest revisions of history lie in three fictitious meetings: two involving Baby and Augusta, and the one involving Augusta and Mrs. McCourt. It is doubtful that Augusta and Baby ever had a face-to-face encounter, but their two scenes together (one in the lobby of the Clarendon Hotel, the other at the ball honoring Horace at the Windsor Hotel) are essential to plot development. Decisions that may have taken Baby months or even years to arrive at are accomplished neatly in fifteen minutes of the Act I scene. Moreover, such a scene could have happened; nothing in the situation or the dialogue is inconsistent with either character. The fact that Augusta and Horace never had an apartment in the Clarendon Hotel is unimportant. Latouche conveniently places her there for her accidental meeting with Baby and the resulting confrontation.

The 1893 meeting at the Windsor Hotel is more of a stretch. Augusta had softened somewhat by that time, but would she have gone to the ball to talk money with Baby? It would have made more sense to have a private meeting in another location, where there would be no danger of Horace interrupting them. For the sake of plot movement, however, that interruption is necessary to establish the "hold on to the Matchless" theme.

The meeting between Mrs. McCourt and Augusta in 1896 is historically impossible because Augusta had died in 1895. Horace's final disaster (the election of McKinley) had to be dealt with, however, and the solution was a very moving scene (for two mezzo sopranos), followed by Augusta's monologue, which has to be one of the great solo scenes in opera.

Another date change is puzzling. Although the Tabor Opera House in Leadville opened in 1879, the date given in the score is 1880. Why the change? The date is never sung, so it could not have been a question of too many syllables. There is probably no way of finding the answer to this question, vexing as it might be to Baby Doe enthusiasts (Doeheads). All of the principals involved in the writing of the opera are dead: Moore, Latouche, Oenslager, and Frank Ricketson—even Caroline Bancroft, a writer of fictitious history, who was always lurking in the wings, itching to be part of the action.

WHY, TOO, IS THE DRUNKEN MINER IN ACT I eventually identified as Jake Sands, owner of the Matchless? Jake Sands, a.k.a. Jacob Sandelowsky, was a dry goods salesman, never owned a mine, and may even have had an affair with the real Baby Doe before she went to Leadville in search of fortune and fame (in that order). In fact, Jake Sands may have been the go-between who introduced Baby to William Bush, Tabor's financial manager, who then arranged a meeting with Horace himself. But a miner? Never!

Tabor did not die on the stage of the Tabor Grand, but death from peritonitis, as the result of a burst appendix, is not very "operatic." Operatically speaking, dying among the memories of his former glories was the way to go.

It is interesting to note that in a film titled *Silver Dollar*, dating from 1932 and starring Edward G. Robinson and Bebe Daniels, the central character, an aging and broken former entrepreneur in Denver named Yates Martin, visits the opera house he had built during his glory days. He sees ghosts from his past and collapses on the stage. He is brought home to his loving wife and dies telling her to hold on to the Matchless Mine. Coincidence? Probably not.

Although the variations from history are interesting, they are of little importance when considering the masterpiece that was the result of the fortunate collaboration of Latouche/Moore. Their treatment goes far beyond the mere historical. Using the story of the Tabors as a springboard and the opening of the mining West as a backdrop, they created a work that has won its place in the operatic repertoire because the piece deals with universal truths and values. In the 1996 house program for Central City Opera I wrote:

> It is a story of undying love (Baby), of suffocating pride (Augusta), of hubris punished by the gods (Horace). Thus the story of Horace and the two Mrs. Tabors becomes Aristotelian in scope, a classic framework reinforced by the vain and frivolous heroine's redemption through love.
>
> We can be moved, of course, by the opera without being aware of its ancient roots. It was the genius of Latouche to construct his tale of the Tabors over a foundation worthy of Greek tragedy. It was the genius of Moore to create a musical score, touching in its simplicity, which provides color, a feeling of period, soaring lyricism and, in the last two scenes, a profound and monumental realization of Latouche's design.

BABY DOE
VERSUS CLIO
The Opera as History

LIO, THE MUSE OF HISTORY, has been well served by *The Ballad of Baby Doe,* but obviously not in the literal sense of historical research and writing. The opera, although well ribbed by history, is not history in the general sense of the scholarly term. It does, nevertheless, tell a story, catch the spirit of the era, and provide a feel for a place and time. Many historical writers fail to appreciate, grasp, or develop successfully these attributes of reliable and readable writing.

Pointing out historical inaccuracies would be easy, and then claiming that they ruin one's appreciation of *The Ballad of Baby Doe* would be equally as facile. In both cases those criticisms would be patently unfair to the opera and what it set out to accomplish. The Tabor story portrays the classic account of Greek tragedy, the rise and fall of a man whose pride—in a nineteenth-century sense—challenged the gods and brought him down. Central City Opera's artistic director emeritus John Moriarty, as mentioned earlier, wrote: "Using the story of the Tabors as a springboard, the opera deals with universal truths and values. It is a story of undying love (Baby's), suffocating pride (Augusta's) and hubris punished by the gods (Horace's). Thus the story of the two Mrs. Tabors becomes Aristotelian in scope, a classic framework reinforced by the vain and superficial heroine's redemption through love."

The intent of the opera has been made explicit in the opera programs over the years and in the foreword to the libretto, the latter included in the two recorded versions that have appeared since its debut. The 1981 Central City Opera House program, *Bravo,* stated, "The warmth of melody and lyric charm that characterize *Baby Doe* also touches deeper, revealing character lines that still run true in our Colorado. Perhaps this is why this love story, embracing as it does the American dream gone wrong, deeply commands our fascination." The original MGM recording (1957) included the following description in its summary of the opera, making *Baby Doe*'s goal even more abundantly clear: "The dramatic treatment of Tabor's life, and the two women who dominated it, closely follows the pattern of fact. Any shifts in the time element and character emphasis have been made to shape the robust chronicle of these into the framework of the musical theater." The 1996 recording reinforced that idea: "Although the opera is accurate in atmosphere, it does differ gently from history, for dramatic purposes sometimes demanded a certain rearrangement of the facts."

Opera, as previously stated, is not history, nor is it intended to be. *Baby Doe* gently dissociates itself from Clio on occasion. Certain historical and literary liberties were taken to match the operatic production requirements. The question becomes whether the opera was true to the essence of the Tabor story. Without question, license was taken to tell the story, with a couple of instances fairly important, some quite minor, and a few pure fabrication.

For example, William Jennings Bryan never came to Leadville during the 1896 campaign, but his doing so creates dramatic opera. He traveled as far west as his home state of Nebraska during his strenuous whirlwind 18,000-mile campaign. Bryan generally stayed east of the Mississippi River, where the election would be won or lost. It did not matter, for Bryan knew Colorado would vote for silver, as it did overwhelmingly. Bryan received more of the popular vote than any Democratic candidate before him. But in the end, he failed to sway enough midwesterners and easterners; nor could the Democrats match the Republican financial campaign chest.

Bryan might not have reached Leadville, but the speech he gives in the opera is right out of his campaign. His famous "Cross of Gold" speech, which swayed the 1896 Chicago Democratic Convention, can be found partly verbatim and partly in ideas he expresses operatically. The reaction of the listeners in Leadville mirrored that of the Chicago delegates.

Of the operatic leads, only Mama McCourt is mostly fictional. Very little is known about Baby Doe's mother or her relationship with her daughter. The lesser leads all represent characteristic types of individuals, not real people.

Baby Doe never, as far as we know, had a one-on-one confrontation with Augusta, even though the opera has two. Both meetings are laced with strong emotions and compassion, part of the high drama of *Baby Doe*. Augusta did live in Denver after the divorce, so a chance encounter was possible.

As mentioned in Chapter 3, Augusta was dead by the time of the 1896 election. Thus Baby Doe's mother could not have made one last forlorn appeal to Augusta to share her fortune to save the Tabors. Augusta had died a proud and wealthy woman the year before, on January 30, 1895, while wintering in Pasadena, California.

As the opera portrays, divorce was scandalous and shocking to proper Victorian middle-class women. Augusta reacted accordingly on hearing the news of the divorce. After the divorce she was very active in the Unitarian Church in Denver, one of its most zealous members and strongest financial supporters. At her home at Seventeenth and Broadway, Augusta sponsored several Strawberry Festivals for the church's benefit; a June 1886 report said "the doors of Mrs. Tabor's beautiful home were thrown hospitably open." Much to their credit, neither Horace nor Augusta stooped to public recriminations about the other after the conclusion of the *Tabor v. Bush* trial. She never carried out the threats she uttered on being told by her friend, "He plans to divorce you": "If he ever tries to divorce me I'll make him rue the day that he was ever born."

On a more minor note, the Tabors were not married twenty-seven years as the opera suggests. At the time of the divorce they were in their twenty-fifth year of marriage, close to their twenty-sixth anniversary. Operatic license was taken for a simple reason: twenty-seven fits the melodic rhythm of the line; twenty-five does not.

Regarding the first divorce, it did take place in Durango (the town), but it is in La Plata County; no Durango County exists in Colorado. Tabor had obtained a divorce there in clandestine proceedings that ended on March 21, 1882. Augusta claimed she was never served a summons. The bailiff said he served the summons, and Bush supported that contention. Interestingly, the pages of the recording books were glued together, and the actual complaint and other pertinent items were missing. Reportedly, Tabor's attorney, Lewis Rockwell, had the items when they were last known; he had also warned Tabor that the divorce was fraudulent.

This was followed in September by the strange St. Louis wedding to Baby Doe that made Tabor a bigamist if the Durango divorce was fraudulent. That affair raised myriad questions that can never be answered without interviewing the two main participants. It all came back to haunt them, though.

Tabor did not die on the stage of the Tabor Grand Opera House, as the opera implies. He died, as mentioned earlier, in the Windsor Hotel, Denver's finest until the opening of the Brown Palace. According to local legend, Tabor's ghost was seen occasionally in the building before it was torn down in 1960.

One other small inaccuracy should be noted: Tabor did not buy the Matchless Mine from Jake Sands. The mine, discovered in June 1878, was sold—in a series of confusing transactions—to a group of investors in August, each of whom sold shares to others. Eventually, in 1879 and 1880, Tabor purchased it. By September of that year, newspapers reported, "Tabor's new bonanza is showing up magnificently." Not, however, before he found himself embroiled in a lawsuit over claim boundaries and partial ownership. This was only one of many lawsuits Horace faced at the height of his prestige and power. The path of wealth and fame proved rocky and full of thorns.

Perhaps the use of the legendary twentieth-century story, that Tabor told Baby Doe to "hang on to the Matchless Mine," does the greatest disservice to history. Nonetheless, it makes for grand opera. As Tabor tells his beloved Baby Doe in Act II, Scene 1, "Then promise me, no matter what happens—you'll always hold on to the Matchless Mine. There's a treasure in the Matchless. You'll keep it always." She promises that she "always" will. That she froze to death at the Matchless adds poignancy but no truth to the story. Like all such legends, this one has a life all its own and has become a treasured part of Colorado folklore.

Where did the tale come from? It would have made a wonderful, touching addition to the stories that appeared during Tabor's final days and after his death. The newspaper coverage seemed almost to be saying that Denver was trying to make amends for not having supported him more during his last years, before he lost his money and property. Perhaps it was an attempt to recapture for a moment a vanished era, the days of fifty-nine, by paying tribute to the man who so strongly represented that long-ago time. Yet there is no mention anywhere that Tabor told Baby Doe to hang on to the Matchless or anything else, for that matter. Nothing so prophetic emerged, for example, in articles in the *Denver Republican, Rocky Mountain News,* and *Denver Post* except these words from Charles Kingsley: "So fleet the works of men."

No mention was made of the Matchless in stories of April 10, 1899, and the days that followed. Only his undeveloped Eclipse Mine near Ward received comment, probably because Horace had recently told a friend, "This is all I've got now, and if it comes up I'll be on the top of the heap again." The sad cadence of his tone, commented the *Post,* "went to the heart of his listener."

Horace did not own the Matchless in 1899, nor did Baby Doe when she lived there in later years. In a bewildering series of transactions long before Horace's death, the Matchless had been mortgaged, leased, involved in lawsuits over title and royalties, and, on paper, sold to several companies with stock sold to the public. Baby Doe lived there only through the intervention of some friends and business associates who purchased the property.

The "hang on to the Matchless" story first appeared in the 1930s. In the midst of the devastating Depression, a ghost from Colorado's legendary nineteenth-century past miraculously materialized. With it came memories of boom times, larger-than-life individuals mastering their destinies, and people in control of their lives. Desperate Coloradans wished all of those things for themselves. It seemed, however, in those dark days that they might never come again.

History provided some hope and release. The Tabors reappeared from out of the mists of Colorado's past. First came David Karsner's book *Silver Dollar* (1932), then the movie *Silver Dollar,* and finally Baby Doe's death at the Matchless Mine in 1935. Twentieth-century Coloradans were reintroduced to the Tabors. The Matchless legend grew out of these events.

Karsner laid the foundation by stating that the dying Tabor told his wife, "Whatever happens, hold on to the Matchless. It will give you back all that I have lost." A few Colorado newspapers picked up the story in the following years. Baby Doe's death at the mine could not have been better timed. It all came together. The *Denver Post* (March 8, 1935), for example, featured the story: "Hold on to the Matchless! former United States Senator H.A.W. Tabor admonished his beautiful wife, Elizabeth (Baby Doe) Tabor, as he lay on his deathbed." Then came the 1937–1938 Tabor serial story, written by Sue Bonnie, which appeared in *True Story Magazine.* Bonnie, a semiliterate prostitute, had lived near Baby Doe during her last years and had been among those who discovered her frozen body. According to Bonnie, the two women had become close friends, and the older woman confided to Sue her intimate life story. "What did she think of the past? Probably I, alone, knew," gushed Bonnie.

Bonnie's tales became the basis for the *True Story* series, which a headline writer tried to make current by writing, "Here is the amazing story of the girl who played the role of Wallis Warfield

[Simpson] in an American Empire." Tabor, however, had not given up his "throne" like Edward VIII to marry the "woman I love"; he had just given up his first wife. In the April 1938 article, Bonnie recounted how the dying Tabor awakened and told his devoted wife, "Never let the Matchless go if I die, Baby. It will make millions again when silver comes back." That story was repeated word for word in Caroline Bancroft's 1950 booklet *Silver Queen,* which even used the same title as the *True Story* series.

Therein lay the key, as the mystery slowly unfolded in the process of finding the guilty party. Bancroft had not plagiarized Bonnie's work because she had written it for a commission, buying the "use of the younger woman's [Bonnie's] name." The magazine required that the story be signed by someone to "whom the subject could have told her life story in the first person." After all, *True Story* proclaimed to its readers, "Truth Is Stranger Than Fiction."

Tracing the story backward proved easy. Bancroft had worked for the *Post* starting in 1928, as book review editor and a historical features writer for the Sunday edition. Karsner acknowledged the help he had received from people at the *Post* in gathering information for his book. Although not specifically named, Caroline's interest in Colorado history was obviously known. The statement might not be conclusive as courtroom evidence, but suspicion certainly pointed toward her. She did say she had talked with the man doing research for the movie *Silver Dollar.*

Was she devious enough to weave fiction into her "histories"? The answer has to be a resounding yes. Among the letters in her 1954–1956 exchange with the Central City Opera House Association, Bancroft, referring to her story of Augusta calling on Baby Doe, admitted that "it is completely fallacious." In a second letter, Caroline revealed another historical "sin" regarding dialogue in *Silver Queen.* She confessed frankly and without apology, "I had *invented* to explain something that I knew to be historically true."

The ultimate missing link finally surfaced in August 1982, when Caroline acknowledged, with some relish and a "twinkle in her eye," that she had fabricated the whole story: "I made it up." Why? "Popular historians must take certain liberties with the truth for the sake of drama." Will the story ever die? Probably not; the legend is too "poignant" not to be believed.

The Ballad of Baby Doe had nothing to do with creating this myth. The opera, however, has unquestionably helped perpetuate the statement "hold on to the Matchless." Caroline Bancroft, beginning with her earlier work, then culminating with her highly romanticized and fictionalized *Silver Queen,* had already executed the historical damage. Caroline had been right when she threatened to sue over her "Tabor" material while the opera was being written. That information had been hers, and with her flight of fancy she created instant "history."

The soap opera approach worked wonderfully; much of the fiction it generated became standard Baby Doe fare in the years following the 1950 publication, combined with later editions. The Tabor story would never be the same. Fairy tales are wonderfully resistant to reality.

The historical significance of *Baby Doe,* though, does not rest with the factual story. Rather, the depiction of the time and place, along with the opera's leading individuals, provides viewers with easy entrance into a long-ago era.

What does *The Ballad of Baby Doe* reflect about mining, the foundation on which the story occurred and is told? Both robustly and gently it gives the listener insight into this industry, as well as into the rise and fall of one of its best-known individuals. Mining is well served.

First and foremost, the initial and last scenes reflect perfectly the familiar boom-and-bust cycles that beset nineteenth-century mining districts and communities. From the boisterous opening in Leadville, with its excitement and eternal optimism, the heart of a mining boom comes into full view. Enthusiastic music and lusty singing successfully portray the era, when all seemed possible and indeed was already happening.

The final scene in Denver's Tabor Grand Opera House is foreboding and dark. The same opening scene musical melodies, here played and sung much differently, take on a different meaning in this atmosphere. Tabor sings a short aria that cuts to the heart of what happened in Colorado, Nevada, and other western mining states. (Remember the aria from Chapter 2.)

How can a man measure himself?
The land was growing, and I grew with it.
In my brain rose buildings yearning towards the sky
And my guts sank deep in the plunging mineshafts
My feet kicked up gold dust wherever I danced
And whenever I shouted my name
I heard a silver echo roar in the wind.

HOW CAN A MINER MEASURE HIMSELF when the district has crashed
and the camp where he once lived and worked has become a
ghost town? Tabor and the chorus, at least in part, answered that
question: "Build me a bank! A big Saloon! Tabor owns the big
hotel. Tabor owns the bank as well. Tabor owns the whole damn
town." Tabor's money helped to develop Leadville and Denver
and points in between. His faith in Colorado led him to shower
the state with enterprises and money, creating jobs and a host of
mining companies and other investments. His actions encouraged
others to come and invest. In fact, he invested in most western
mining states. "Where the big fish go, the small fish will follow."
They did. Tabor and Leadville turned Colorado mining around
after the problems of the 1860s and early 1870s. By 1880, Colorado was America's number-one mining state.

   The life and expectations of the miner are briefly portrayed, as
opposed to those of the owner, which Tabor had become by the
time the opera was written. In the opening scene, Tabor sings with
his four cronies about their lives before the big silver strikes.

I dug by day and dug by starlight.
I'm an honest son of labor
Dug my way right through to Hell.
Satan said "why here comes Tabor!"

Dig you gophers
Dig them holes
Dig away to save your souls
More buckets of gold than banks can hold
Lie deep in Colorado.

Dig away to save your souls
When the chips are all down
You'll wear a silver crown
Right here in Colorado

When the chips are down
You'll put on a crown
Right here in Colorado.

If not all the way to hell, they dug nevertheless, and many found their "silver crown" right in Colorado. In the end, they contracted nearly incurable gold fever and silver fever, both of which can be terminal. Whether "deadly" or not, both fevers affected miners in almost everything they did.

In another verse of the aria Tabor says, "Took the devil for my partner." Considering the vicissitudes, unknowns, and physical dangers of mining, it would not be far-fetched for some miners to think they had the devil for a partner—or to wish they had. Mining and miners could not "see beyond the pick at the end of the drift" in the nineteenth century, which made the odds against success even greater. The more whimsical ones believed tommy knockers, those mysterious inhabitants of mines who had seemingly migrated from Cornwall, charted their fate.

These nineteenth-century miners had pride in their profession and in what they had accomplished in developing the West. This idea comes through clearly when Tabor sings "We're the ones who built this land and we're going to run it or know the reason why." Mining was the foundation for settlement, promotion, and development in three Rocky Mountain states—Colorado, Montana, and Idaho.

In the blink of an eye, the mining West turned into an urban West. That development has proved eternally fascinating. In a sense, tourists and residents fascinated each other. The former enjoyed seeing the "zoo" and maybe sampling some of the "sin." The latter enjoyed seeing these strangers and how they behaved.

The lifestyle of the mining towns is briefly glimpsed in the opening of Act I, as Tabor and his friends celebrate the opening of Leadville's opera house. The music sets an excited, busy tempo. Optimism is in the air. "It's a bang-up job," sings Tabor about his opera house. "Yes sir, it's a fittin' place for art and culture. We can use some culture here in Colorado." Augusta admonishes her husband, "Can't you manage to cooperate in our efforts to provide some change of tone in this money-grubbing town—some touch of beauty and refinement?" Horace's response is revealing: "Dollars from that old saloon same as dollars from the mines helped to build that handsome opry house—helped to put this shindig on."

The typical mining town showed both attitudes—the desire to develop and get rich and a yearning for art and culture. In real life many, including the Tabors, desired something beyond the materialism of the era and the industry. Leadville might have been grander and more exuberant than most of its contemporaries, but it mirrored on a larger scale the aspirations of a generation of mining folk.

A central theme of the opera is the impact of wealth on individuals. Horace and Augusta generally responded in different ways. After complaining that her husband had documents, stocks, bonds, invoices, and bills all "jumbled helterskelter" on his desk, she finds a check to buy the Matchless Mine: "Lorda-mighty, no! He wants to buy another mine! The man's idiotic." Tabor did not think so. His decades-long grubstaking had finally paid off handsomely. Augusta might not have liked the bad debts their books carried because he grubstaked scores of prospectors, but his faith in mining proved boundless. It only took one Little Pittsburg to redeem a host of poor investments.

Tabor's faith in both mining and himself guided his career. He ultimately built an empire that included mines, opera houses, a stagecoach line, property, banks, and a host of other investments. They led him into eventual financial decline, but he never lost faith in himself, in Denver, and in Colorado. The same could be said of other mining men throughout the West, including, for example, the Comstock's Big Four, Butte's copper kings, and legions of lesser-known individuals.

Fortunes affected many lifestyles in ways similar to Tabor's. The sudden acquisition of large amounts of money has a way of changing people—their spending habits, their morals, their very way of life. As the Greek philosopher Sophocles warned more than 2,000 years earlier, "Money. There's nothing in the world so demoralizing as money." For Tabor and some other successful mining men, that warning proved apt. The willingness to enjoy money with reckless abandon was not unusual, nor was the desire to build monuments to their name and fame. As Denver newspaperman and poet Eugene Field wrote upon the glorious opening of the Tabor Grand Opera House, "The opera house, a union grand of capital and labor; long will the stately structure stand, a monument to Tabor."

Sowing one's wild oats later in life also seems to have been fairly common among the suddenly wealthy mining magnates and others. Flings involving older men and younger women happened so often that they created little comment unless publicized. Augusta knew much about her husband's wanderings. As she told Baby Doe in their first meeting in the opera, "I suppose he's told you that there have been others?" Baby Doe protested, "Yes, he has. But what I feel is different from women like that." Augusta did not think so.

The deterioration of Horace's marriage to Augusta started long before the silver wealth, as was described in an earlier chapter, but Leadville's bonanza cut the final cords. The opera portrays the problems and stresses vividly and, as far as can be ascertained, truthfully. Augusta had aged, bringing out more strongly some of her New England heritage. She did not enjoy the wealth and social/political whirl into which they had rushed following their silver bonanza; Tabor enjoyed it enormously. That allowed a side of his personality to be revealed, one that had always been there except that their circumstances and Augusta had kept it repressed. The second time he met Baby Doe he sang with candor:

> And while I was listening [Baby Doe had just finished the
> Willow aria]
> I was recalling all the things
> Things that once I had wanted so much
> And forgotten as years slipped away
> A girl I knew back home in Vermont
> The sea in New Hampshire
> The first sight of the mountains.
> They say I've been lucky
> There's nothing my money won't buy
> It couldn't be I was unhappy
> Or was missing the good things of life.

Augusta, the astute businesswoman, left the marriage with a fortune and loneliness. Tabor went on to fame, scandal, and legend, despite a sad end to his empire. The public liked this type of story in the nineteenth century, as it still does, and many wealthy mining men provided grist for the newspapers and tabloids.

The idea of divorce stunned Augusta in life as well as in the opera, as mentioned previously. The woman's role as mother and wife was sacred in Victorian America. The fact that she opposed a divorce was easily understood considering her middle-class New England background. In this era of double standards, men could sow their wild oats; the wife, if the marriage failed, often received the blame. The role of the wife was to preserve the sacredness of marriage, and Augusta was not about to fail in that role if she could possibly help it.

It is plausible that Augusta might have thought of her husband as "a weakling, too big for his britches." She had been a strong pillar in their marriage and, as Samuel Leach observed in his Buckskin Joe letters, the harder-working of the two, a "driver." As Tabor had admitted to Leach, "I have to be prodded." Tabor enjoyed leisure much more than she did, and Augusta clearly had to keep him going at times.

Contrasting Augusta, the businesswoman, with Baby Doe, the pretty "gold digger," has long made for popular fare. In the second of their operatic meetings, Baby Doe confesses to Augusta, "I have no head for business." This sentiment makes for good opera and clearly contrasts the two, but it is not true. Baby Doe helped with Horace's business dealings through the troubled 1890s, especially when Horace was away in Mexico in his last-ditch effort to find a paying mine. She has to be given a great deal of credit during the crucial years 1893–1894. Separated from her husband much of the time and under increasing creditor pressure, Baby Doe strove to maintain Tabor's holdings in Colorado. Their hope in Mexico failed, and that left the Tabors desperately praying for salvation by the government's raising the price of silver.

As Augusta correctly pointed out in the last meeting with Baby Doe in the opera, "Why, child, he's mortgaged to the hilt! His fortune is on paper—everyone knows that. The price of silver is half what it was ten years ago, but still I read of nothing but his extravagances." Silver's price had not dropped by half, but it was falling fast. Meanwhile, Horace's mines, deeper and with lower-grade ore, were not producing as they once had, facts exacerbated by the higher costs of the deep mining. Tabor's faith in Colorado and himself had led to an investment frenzy in the 1880s, a frenzy that became more reckless when no new Little Pittsburgs appeared.

A turning point for the opera, as it was for mining, proved to be the silver issue. Basically, the metal was being overproduced against lessening use, resulting in a falling silver price. Miners and westerners, as discussed in Chapter 1, did not look at the situation in this black-and-white economic fashion. They blamed plots concocted by bankers, foreigners, big business, easterners, the federal government, and almost anyone else who came to mind.

Silver had made Colorado the number-one mining state and had underwritten its expansion and prosperity for a dozen years. The declining price, down from $1.35 an ounce to the 90-cent range, grew more serious as the 1880s neared their end. Neither the Republican nor the Democratic Party responded to cries for help from the silver states—they wanted a guaranteed price and the government to purchase silver. They received help through federal purchases of silver and coinage of silver dollars, but no guaranteed price was established.

The result created a new political realignment in Colorado, as mentioned previously. The new Populist Party, or People's Party, adopted "Free Silver" as part of its reform platform, a platform that wanted to return power to the people. Colorado voted Populist in 1892. Meanwhile, Tabor's declining fortunes were sharply etched against the collapse of silver. Horace had placed his fate on that of silver, as he told Baby Doe at the governor's ball: "Silver will rise, and we will rise with it."

That provided the background for Tabor's confrontation with his four cronies in Act II, Scene 2. Although they are talking about the 1896 campaign, in reality they are discussing a situation that had been steadily escalating for two decades. Tabor warns them, "We can't take it lying down. This country is a sight too big to be run by a bunch of brokers from New York." His four friends, who unlike most Coloradans had stayed loyal to the business-dominated Republicans, advised him, "If you can't beat 'em, join 'em." They counseled Horace, "The wind won't blow our way again. Not like it used to."

For them and for the Republicans in the 1890s, that was the wrong path to take in Colorado. Tabor and his generation were fed up with what they considered unsympathetic, powerful outsiders and their seeming control of Colorado's fortunes and destiny. "Don't knuckle under to those Eastern moneybags!" Horace stubbornly replies. "There's a great man rising out of the West. He speaks for men like us—Bryan, William Jennings Bryan." The politically weak West was looking for a Moses to lead it, and it found him in 1896.

Then, in one of opera's high emotional points, Tabor turns on his erstwhile friends, who had been with him from the start. In that moment the tension, the crisis, and Tabor's plight are caught forever. Tabor replies:

> Turn tail and run, then!
> Forget when you worked the mines,
> Dug the dirt with bare hands
> To build the place you stand on.
> To keep that little pinch of earth
> You've cornered for your own
> You're willing to be lackeys!
> Well, there's free men still, who ain't scared,
> The whole country over!
>
> It's you who are the turncoats—
> Silver made you what you are.

The election of 1896 would tell the story, a fact generally recognized by voters during the campaign. The Republican Party stood foursquare behind gold and nominated William McKinley. Meanwhile, the Democrats selected Nebraska's silver-tongued orator, William Jennings Bryan, and silver, and they stole most of the rest of the Populist platform. As Tabor said at Leadville's rally for Bryan:

McKinley's dogs have had their day
'cause silver ore is here to stay
Let the merchants understand
We're the ones who built this land
and we're going to run it
Or know the reason why.

It was debtor versus creditor, easterner versus westerner, goldbug versus silverite, rich versus poor, urbanite versus ruralite in a struggle for America's heart and future. Logic went out the window. Emotion came in to stay.

Bryan, as he had during the campaign, returned to these themes in the imaginary Leadville speech, calling the miners "the sinews of our nation's strength." The "armor of a righteous cause" made the humblest citizen more powerful than the "hosts of error." His listeners well understood that meant bankers, Republicans, eastern and foreign investors, and anyone who opposed Free Silver. "Drive the money changers from the temples of our land. Renew the ancient covenant between mankind and God"—that was the challenge with which he closed while his listeners chanted "Bryan, Bryan, Bryan."

Defiant, dedicated, determined—the silverites stood for their cause, their man. The opera catches a clear sense of the era, the people. The music, the lyrics, and the chorus and soloists all mirror the temper of the times. Hope stood framed against desperation.

You miners, doctors and you cow-pokes
You city clerks and farming folks
You're not deaf and dumb and blind
Now it's time to speak your mind!
Tell it to the nation upon election day!

They told the nation, but the nation did not hear. McKinley won.

Instantly, the opera takes on a new tone. Desperation turns to despair, an era has ended, the new industrial/urbanized America has triumphed. The twentieth century waited just around the corner. Tabor and his age slipped into history and legend. Horace could only reflect back on what had been or what might have been.

"How can a man measure himself?" he asks pleadingly. The words of the English poet Charles Kingsley, which Tabor had inscribed on the drop curtain of the Tabor Grand Opera House, take on that haunted message discussed in Chapter 1:

> So fleet the works of men
> Back to the earth again;
> Ancient and holy things
> Fade like a dream.

Tabor never intended these words to be an epitaph for himself or for nineteenth-century mining; nevertheless, they could serve as such, both in the opera and in real life.

The Ballad of Baby Doe recaptures an era as few other accounts have. The time, the place come alive; it is hoped that the spirit and vigor of *Baby Doe* will cultivate interest among its audiences to pursue the era further. If so, the question of the despondent Tabor has been answered: "Ain't there something, someone, somewhere, sometime, that somehow I can hold onto?" In the end, neither he nor Augusta nor Baby Doe will be forgotten. The measurement of a man can indeed be assessed.

THE BALLAD OF BABY DOE AT CENTRAL CITY
A Photographic Essay

FOLLOWING THE WORLD PREMIERE on Saturday, July 7, 1956, *Baby Doe* has been performed during six seasons at Central City. The first of the subsequent performances occurred during the centennial celebration of the Pikes Peak gold rush in 1959. Appropriately, the Tabors came west in 1859. That season was followed with performances of the opera in 1966 and again during the state's centennial in 1976. It was also performed in 1981 (the opera's silver anniversary), 1988, and 1996.

The opera gained in popularity, not only in Colorado but throughout the country, and it has even been sung abroad. The story of the Tabors lives on, rising beyond itself to become legendary to viewers who will never see Fryer Hill or the Matchless Mine.

It has gathered loyal fans, Doeheads, throughout the land and even has its own website. *Baby Doe* might even have been able to convince that onetime westerner Mark Twain to enjoy opera. Twain was never comfortable with opera, observing: "I dislike the opera because I want to love it and can't."

What follows is a tour down memory lane with *Baby Doe* at Central City. Later comes the cast for each season; first a photographic journey through the opera. Each season is represented, as are all the scenes of the opera. Remember and enjoy.

(All photographs courtesy of the Central City Opera House Association unless otherwise noted.)

"I came this way from Massachusetts, through the Kansas Territory, pick and shovel in my hand, belly full of gin and glory." (1966 Production)

"Dig you gophers, dig them holes, dig away to save your souls." (1966
Production)

"I beg your pardon, can you direct me to the Clarendon Hotel?" (1966 Production)

"Gone are the ways of pleasure, gone are the friends I had of yore." (1956 Production)

"Things that once I had wanted so much and forgotten, as years slipped away. A girl I knew back home in Vermont, the sea in New Hampshire, the first sight of the mountains." (1959 Production)

"Give me those gloves! So you've been seeing her!" "What if I have?" (1988 Production; courtesy, Mark Kiryluk)

"I'll save your time and mine by telling you, frankly, I know all about you, about you and Horace." (1981 Production)

"You're not going, my heart, my breath, my pulse! All that is bountiful, beautiful, heavenly." (1959 Production)

"Divorce! Not on your life! I am Mrs. Tabor, there ain't any other." (1981 Production)

"Senator and Mrs. Horace Tabor. Ah! Ah! Enchanting! Beautiful! Lovely! Charming!" (1956 Production)

"For my beloved bride, a queen among women." (1996 Production; courtesy, Mark Kiryluk)

"Gold is a fine thing for those who admire it. Gold is like the sun, but I am a child of the moon, and silver is the metal of the moon." (1976 Production)

"What are you doing here? Is it not enough to turn half the town against me? Must you turn my darling against me as well?" (1976 Production)

"Here, throw these in the pot, this gold and these jewels—place my bet on silver along with yours." (1981 Production)

"McKinley and his big-time backers want to knock the props from under silver."
(1959 Production)

"Who is Mr. Bryan, Mummy?" "Mr. Bryan is a very great man. A champion of the people." (1988 Production; courtesy, Mark Kiryluk)

"Let the merchants understand, we're the ones who built this land, and we'll run it or know the reason why." (1996 Production; courtesy, Mark Kiryluk)

*"Bryan, Bryan, Bryan! We are marching to glory with our banners waving."
(1976 Production)*

"That's all very noble. And it helps you to hold on to your dollars. Dollars that Tabor gave you, too!" (1988 Production; courtesy, Mark Kiryluk)

"Augusta! Augusta! How can you turn away? He was so dear to you when you promised always to cherish him." (1981 Production)

"Build me a bank! A big saloon! Goin' to be governor, maybe president!" (1981 Production)

"And you'll remember me? Always and forever?" (1988 Production; courtesy, Mark Kiryluk)

"I shall walk beside my love who is husband, father, child." (1996 Production; courtesy, Mark Kiryluk)

Curtain call. (1976 Production)

6

WRITING DESK AND BACKSTAGE

A Glimpse into *Baby Doe* as It Was Composed and Sung

WHEN *THE BALLAD OF BABY DOE* was suffering through the pangs of birth, Douglas Moore taught at Columbia and served as head of his department, which during those years glowed as a "hotbed" of American opera. Only one of several composers who taught there at the time, the kindly Moore was given credit for being "encouraging and supportive to a lot of young composers, young American composers."

There seems little question that Moore discussed the project with some of his colleagues, and they aided him with "bits and pieces" of the opera. Beatrice Krebs, who sang at Central City in 1956, in a later interview claimed Richard Rodgers had helped Moore with the score, and Emerson Buckley had added some of the honky-tonk for the last scene.

Moore's longtime friend, fellow composer and Columbia University professor Jack Beeson, contributed further insights into the writing of *Baby Doe.* One of Moore's protégés and a frequent visitor to his home, Beeson offered an insider's view. He related that he and Moore had "played scenes to each other" from their various compositions, including *Baby Doe,* and would "trade ideas." Beeson stated that he helped his friend with orchestration, which he felt "Moore wasn't very good at." Agreeing with Krebs in part, Beeson said he also helped with some melodic ideas, including the jazz riff in "Come Down Moonshine" for Silver Dollar in the final scene.

John Latouche also received some assistance. Miles Kreuger, a writer and close friend of Latouche, commented, "He needed somebody to help him because he was, well, to put it modestly, terribly disorganized." Beeson called Latouche simply "undisciplined" and said Moore sometimes had to "lock him up" to get something written. Kreuger praised Latouche highly despite his dilatory habits.

> The lyrics in *Baby Doe* reveal so much about character and about era and about social values, and they are more than just moon/June lyrics and even [than] lyrics that move the plot forward. You really come to know those people [the Tabors]. You come to know them, what they think and what they feel and who they are. The lyrics also separate people by age. The characters clearly have different ages. Mrs. Tabor and Baby Doe don't sing the same kind of lyrics because one is older and one is younger. That's a very subtle point, too, I think.

Leyna Gabriele had gotten to know Moore while she was at Columbia University. The "courtly gentleman" needed to find a "silvery soprano [to] hear how those high notes would work and how the whole thing would work." Her voice teacher suggested Leyna learn the part as he was writing it. That was how she got involved, and it led to her singing the role in the first Central City season.

Like many others, she believes Augusta "is the strongest part in the opera." Leyna had an interesting interpretation as to why. She believes Douglas was "enamored" with Baby Doe and did not want to show her "conniving" to capture Horace. Latouche, on the other hand, was "enamored" with Augusta, "so he really wrote very strongly for her."

There was no question that Moore's and Latouche's work habits were dramatically opposed, the highly disciplined, regularly working composer compared with an erratic lyricist who produced in fits and bursts. Moore commented in an interview, "In *The Ballad of Baby Doe* it was a funny arrangement. Latouche was always disappearing. He was always busy. I was so excited that I would go ahead and write" (meaning the words).

Douglas Moore's two daughters, Sarah and Mary, discussed memories of their father's composing of the opera. Both liked John Latouche, Sarah saying, "John must never have [had] a dull moment in his life, because no person is dull to him." Mary concurred, "He was a lively person; John was just enchanting." They thought that although he was the ideal person to work with, Latouche was slow in finishing the lyrics. Moore always used the "lyrics to establish the pattern of the music." Both agreed, however, that in the case of the "Willow Song," "he wrote the lyrics and the music before John had caught up with him, but that wasn't like the ordinary."

The story of Baby Doe and her death at the Matchless seemed to be Moore's window to the West. It haunted him. "Other than Baby Doe," Sarah believed, "he never . . . struck me as being particularly a western buff." She continued, "He was really always more interested in women's parts because they were more fun to write than men's parts in opera, and you had two such good roles in Baby Doe and Augusta."

Mary told an engaging and revealing story of the two men working together to revise the opera after the July 1956 performances.

> They decided to revise it and add some things, and there was
> a song in the opera scene that begins the second act called
> "Wake Snakes," which Baby sang. It was a nice vivacious
> song, but it had no relevance to the opera. John then wrote,
> at Daddy's insistence, the song "The Fine Ladies Walk." But
> I remember his being down in the country, and he was
> staying with us, and he wasn't writing it, and Daddy was

very anxious to get it, you know. It was the summer, he
wanted to get it written while he had time to do it. So John
was upstairs. He actually was shut in his room thinking, and
we all quietly began cocktails. We were halfway through
when suddenly John appeared on the stage with a yell of a
wounded animal and said, "You started without me."

Speaking of her father brought to Sarah's mind the problems
of teaching and composing: "Daddy could really work in a con-
centrated way in the summers. He could do orchestrations in the
winter, but when he was working at Columbia, he couldn't do
much in the way of composing." They were all "very much aware"
of *Baby Doe* when it was being developed. Her father would try
things out "when he'd first written them; I can remember everybody sort of talking with him and John, for instance, on the silver
song. I was saying that I thought that Baby Doe would particularly like silver because she was a nighttime person, as opposed to
a daytime person. John liked the idea very much, and he went
back and wrote the silver song." The result became the wedding
aria in which Baby Doe sings, "But I am a child of the moon, and
silver is the metal of the moon."

An excited Sarah traveled to Central City for the premiere.
"The whole high quality of Central City was kind of heady. It
was very festive." Her dad was "very happy, really happy. It was
exciting then, too," because there were hopes of having the show on
Broadway. Moore, however, "never felt it was right for Broadway."

Jack Beeson, on the other hand, thought it was written in
Broadway fashion, with its short scenes. It had, he felt, a "lot of
musical comedy, except, of course, [for] the subject matter." This
was not to demean *Baby Doe,* in his mind. He loved the way Moore
developed American subjects, used "old music" as models, and
upheld the opera's tuneful nature: "It doesn't confront listeners
with sounds they are unaccustomed to."

Allen Young, who observed the opera in rehearsal and on
stage in 1956 and several times thereafter, offered some interesting
insights into Emerson Buckley, who conducted the opening season as well as the New York recording. Young believed Buckley
was very charming and "a very good conductor." There were

problems, however, because *Baby Doe* was not a traditional opera, and the cast had not had many "opportunities to sing other than traditional operas." Buckley "worked on the actors" to get them ready. Emerson "could be cantankerous and really wanted the singers to pay attention to him." Occasionally, he could be "particularly hard on a singer, almost terribly vindictive." Buck would almost "ream a singer out." Yet Young asserted in a 1999 interview, "Buckley was the right person to bring *Baby Doe* to Central City."

Following its premiere in Central City in 1956, *The Ballad of Baby Doe* went on to New York in 1958, with Beverly Sills singing Baby Doe. Again it received rave reviews, with Sills highly praised for her interpretation and "fire." The *New Yorker* (April 1958) described the opera as "a very important event in the history of music, it is both a genuine opera and a genuine expression of our peculiarly American way of looking at things—one that Moore has proved is as normal, natural, and thoroughly enjoyable as anything else in the contemporary theater." *Opera News* joined the salute, praising its music, which "breathes honest sentiment," and its charming succession of arias, ensembles, and choruses. The review, however, was critical of the last scenes and particularly "the long-winded, misplaced dream sequence." *Baby Doe* was selected by the Critics' Circle Awards as the best new opera produced in New York that season. *The Ballad of Baby Doe* had come a long way in two years and was only getting started.

Beginning with the 1956 production, a host of people have sung the opera's various roles. Their reactions to the opera and their role in it are part of *Baby Doe*'s history. Except for Beverly Sills, who never performed the role at Central City, all of the individuals interviewed for this book sang there in *Baby Doe*. Credit for preserving much of this heritage, which would otherwise have been lost, goes to one of the most devoted Doeheads, David Kanzeg, who in the 1990s located as many people as possible who had sung the leads in *Baby Doe*. His enthusiasm and dedication deserve a standing ovation from all who love the opera.

In the 1956 and 1966 productions and also in the 1958 MGM recording, Frances Bible sang Augusta. She remembered how she first became acquainted with *Baby Doe:* "I was just called and asked, would I like to do it in Central City, and, of course, I said yes. I didn't know what it was all about at that point, and then I started looking into the history and getting books to read and that sort of thing." After rehearsing in New York City, Bible came to Central City and met a lawyer whose father had been one of Tabor's lawyers. He had photographs of the Tabors, and she was pleased to find that slender Augusta had "been a very handsome woman" when younger. "She became stiff and austere looking, but originally on their trip across the country, she looked quite young and lovely."

Frances Bible came to admire a "very religious and proper" Augusta, whose New England heritage equaled her own. "Coming from that part of the country myself, it helped me a little to understand the character." New England people "don't show their emotions" openly, and thus she found the role of Augusta taxing "because the emotion is all held inside."

> Originally, the part of Augusta was written for a dramatic soprano, and then the composer decided that he wanted a little heavier voice than that in the part, but he didn't rewrite the part. So it is quite taxing. It gets up on top quite a lot, you know, and he didn't rewrite any of the high notes to fit the lower voice. So it's quite dramatic, especially the scene with the friends of Augusta. For me, that's the high point. Although the last aria that she does, she's torn between whether she should go and help him or whether she shouldn't, and she decides not to, and that's her last appearance in the opera— it's very dramatic.

Her first reaction was to feel sorry for Augusta, which "I still do, but I imagine that both of them were hard to live with." Of Horace and Baby Doe she said, "I'll tell you one thing, both of them were notorious for their extracurricular activities, and once they met and fell in love, neither one of them ever looked at anybody else after that, so I guess it was a real true love affair." Asked about her favorite section of the opera, Bible replied, "Well, I think a very effective thing is at the end, when the snow starts to fall." That last aria successfully covers the years between 1899 and 1935 and leaves the audience with strong feelings, she concluded.

Toward the end of the interview, Bible made some fascinating observations on critics and their reviews. She also offered several perceptive insights into "appreciating *Baby Doe.*"

> I remember when the critics first came out and saw *Baby Doe.* Typically, they didn't like it. They just generally didn't think much of it. Then all of a sudden it became the in thing, and now it won the Critics Award and all this stuff. I think they always just have to say, we don't like it. I don't see how you can decide you like anything on one hearing, which is all they had to start with. I think that if they really were serious, they would come and they would look at the score. They would see it two or three times and then write a review. How can you judge something on hearing it one time, because *Baby Doe* grows on you. I think the fact that it sort of has little snatches of this and that—folksy—turns them off at first, but you begin to realize the point of it after you've lived with it awhile, and it does pull on you, it grows on you, which is a good sign.

Walter Cassel sang with Bible in 1956 and on the 1958 recording. His Horace became the standard by which others would be judged for years. He, too, commented about *Baby Doe,* especially the criticism that it was not really an opera but more of a Broadway production.

> I think those that claim that don't know what they are talking about. This was a strange part of it. When we did *Baby Doe* in Central City, some of the New York critics came out for that, but they didn't think it was very great. I think their observations were rather shallow.
>
> There's a way to listen and a way not to listen, too, as well as a way to sing. They began to change their opinions and see that there was some real depth in Horace Tabor, Baby Doe, and the whole Tabor family.
>
> It's about American people, about American habits, the thing they loved, silver, and also a little gold thrown in. It's really the heart and soul, I think, of America, and why not fall in love with the thing that they grew up with and nurtured and loved and still love.

He ended by saying, "If your observation is not deep enough, how can you observe deeply? It's just as simple as that."

Regarding his introduction to the opera, Cassel had an interesting story. His manager told him that a composer (Douglas Moore) "wants to talk with you about possibly being interested in an opera called *The Ballad of Baby Doe*."

> So I went up to Doug's apartment, and he played through some of it. I don't know whether you've ever heard Doug play the piano. I must admit I couldn't tell what he thought he was playing. He plays almost like sketchiness, you know how some composers sketch notes. The piano hadn't been tuned for years. I had to be tactful and ask for the music. I couldn't tell, and I took the score home. We [his accompanist and Cassel] went over and just fell in love with it, and the result was that we wanted to be part of it. So Doug Moore was happy about that. I went to Central City where we did it, and we were so carried away with the opera.
>
> It kind of sang itself, the Horace Tabor part. It was so naturally written. There was a little rewriting done after we left Central City but before we played it in the New York City Opera. But basically, it was there.

"The more we heard it, the more we liked the opera," Cassel concluded. "To me it's a masterpiece, and I know it takes people time, some people it takes more time than others. But if you have any taste and adventure in your heart, you are going to be carried away with this opera, especially when it's well done. We had a good, good cast in Central City there." He credited Hanya Holm, "who was superb," for bringing the best out in the performers: "She knew how to draw every ounce of blood out of us, and the blood that belonged in the opera, and, well, it felt like we were turning into the people we were supposed to be playing."

Cassel clearly understood what the allure of *Baby Doe* meant to him, other singers, and a large portion of the listeners: "It gets into your skin, and you become part of it because it's real, part of it is really real. You can't escape it. These are human lives you are dealing with. It's true, the singing and the thinking all get tied together, or should, if they are completely wed and happy."

Having sung Horace in *Baby Doe* probably a hundred times, Cassel explained further: "I lived it. I felt like I did anyway. To live something means you have to put your blood flowing through it. You have to become it, you have to forget that you are Cassel. You know, it's not easy. It's like hypnotizing. Well, the opera is hypnotic. I don't know how you feel about it, but part of Doug Moore and Latouche are all there, too." He especially enjoyed the aria "Warm as the Autumn Light," which was added after the Central City premiere, for its "changes of mood, thought, and pace." The singer has to understand the man and the mood; "it lends great depth, and when that's not there you miss much of Moore's beautiful music and story." The same insights were true, he felt, for the last scene.

Cassel did admit that although he usually liked doing research about an opera in which he was about to perform, this time he did not: "We went right into the opera so fast, I didn't have the time." With two casts needing to be prepared, he thought they rehearsed about four weeks for the opening night in 1956.

Claire Jones, who sang the role of one of Augusta's four friends in 1956, joyously recalled that summer. Commenting about the rehearsals, she noted:

> Dr. Moore was very low-key, very sweet. He's one of those men that you meet that is goodness but very strong. [Emerson Buckley] is a bit overpowering at times—and many conductors are. Dr. Moore would walk up to him and just touch him on the shoulder, and his sweet, gentle manner would get exactly what he wanted; he never raised his voice.
> John Latouche was just a delightful man, and he was very undemanding about everything. It was very important to him that every word was distinct because he said, "I didn't put those words down just to amuse myself." Then he'd laugh, because he's just a fun man. He would be out square dancing with us in the streets and everything, and he was just a wonderful man.
> Moore and Latouche were there for everything. Emerson was conducting everything. He was really busy. Latouche was very private, no one ever got too close to him. Dr. Moore was private, but he was warm and also open.

Fresh out of school, Claire thought it would be wonderful to sing in the opera at Central City: "You know, I was nineteen and very astute!" Others, though, were concerned about the effect of

the altitude on them and their voices: "They found out the altitude really affected the singers more than they thought, the ones
from the Met. I was a young person, didn't worry at all about my
voice. I just thought, I'm strong, and I'll just bellow out anything." While there, she also was the understudy for Mama
McCourt and sang in that season's companion opera, *Tosca*. "We
did eight performances a week; we did four *Baby Does* and four *Toscas*."

If that was not enough, Claire gained another responsibility.
Martha Lipton had trouble with the altitude: "The choral director walked up to me and said, 'Emerson wondered if you would
learn Augusta's role. Since you are on stage with her a lot, why
don't you just learn it also.' I just looked at him, and I thought
okay, but I was young. I didn't know any of this when I went
there. I thought I was just going to sing chorus."

Claire Jones had fond memories of her "wonderful" summer
at Central City: "We rehearsed, of course, in the opera house and
ate our meals, most of them, in the Teller House right next door.
We'd all congregate in that bar at the Teller House and sing all
night. We'd finish the show and get dressed and go over there and
sing. At that time *My Fair Lady* had just opened on Broadway,
and so everybody was singing everything from *My Fair Lady*."

As for the cast (except the leads), "We all just kind of lived
like a big family. We all lived in separate houses up and down that
hill. Most of the guys lived about one block up, and the women
lived about two blocks up the hill." Although Claire was not a
morning person, she and several friends would get up early and
wander around the hills: "That was really our only free time. So
some of the musicians in the orchestra would bring their instru-
ments, and a couple of violinists would come along, bring their
violins, and we'd be up there at 6:00 in the morning listening to
violins. Occasionally, Dr. Moore would come with us. Walter
Cassel came."

She remembered as well the "grand and glorious" premiere
night: "We knew that we had a great hit, and the people were just
ecstatic [on] opening night when the curtains went down. They
stood and just yelled. It wasn't polite clapping at all. It was just
bravo, bravo. That's not normal in Central City."

They had this big ball in the Teller House. The Teller House was decked out in its finest array, and there was a big ball there, and we danced. Up and down the streets they had a lot of entertaining. Waiters and things, in the restaurants and in the different places, had worked these square dances and Virginia reels. Latouche was out there with them; he loved to square dance.

Life magazine was there and all the (there were many) many reporters. Yes, at that time I was so young and green, and flashlights were going off all the time. And the leads, Dolores [Wilson] and Walter [Cassel] were just, well, they looked [like] a king and queen. Everybody was just in awe of them.

Claire, too, sensed the opera was something significant: "Yes, yes, yes, I thought, how did I luck into this, and I thought, gosh, what a great experience it was. I'm right out of a small conservatory, had never done anything."

Beatrice Krebs sang Mama McCourt that premiere evening, as well as in 1966 and on the 1958 recording. With a bit of humor, she remembered that "musically there was no problem," but that one of the biggest problems "for the role was the 6-foot train." Hanya Holm staged it so "she wanted me to turn completely around. So I was caught in this train, and then she showed me that all I had to do was step over it . . . behind me again. But that took a lot of practicing." The stage was not very big, and just before her entrance "they would arrange my train on the steps very artistically, so it made a nice picture to open with, and it was fun. It was a fun role."

Krebs continued to talk about that train and the marriage scene: "For that particular scene (this was the first opera that Hanya had staged, and it was one which had a lot of people in it), I swear we must have done it at least seventeen times in one way. She came in one morning and said, 'Well now, I see what I want to do,' and changed it all. We did it from then on in another way."

Regarding the role of Mama McCourt, Krebs pointed out, "The woman obviously wasn't written to have good sense. Basically, in all the stories of Baby Doe she was fictional because she didn't show [up] in the histories, and Latouche put her in that way." Her costume was "fantastic, and it had two wired big hoops over each shoulder, sleeveless, and it was a beautiful French lace appliqué over the top."

Krebs had been warned about possible negative effects of the altitude and "knew that would be a problem, but I had a very long breath line in my singing." She jokingly said, "There was oxygen available." She continued, "In some cases I sort of thought it became an excuse, but you did have to make that original adjustment."

Life was routine for the cast—the Teller House, as always, for meals, and "a lot of rehearsals were done across the street [at Williams Stables], where they ended up doing the barn dancing, folk dancing, and that sort of thing." There was not, Krebs felt, "a whole lot extra to do there," but Leyna Gabriele (alternate Baby Doe) had a car. Like many visitors to mountainous areas, "She didn't particularly like to drive it, especially in the mountains." So Beatrice and several other female cast members would drive for her. "We would go out and tour around and see the various areas and that sort of thing."

Unlike some of her contemporaries, Krebs did not sense the opera might be something special: "No, not quite that much, no. I was delighted, needless to say." Yet she caught the excitement of opening night: "Well, it was exciting. Of course, Mama McCourt doesn't come in until the 6th scene [Act I], so I could hear excitement building in the whole plot up until then."

Beverly Sills seemed an ideal choice when she was selected to sing Baby Doe in the New York production in 1958. Commenting on the role, she observed:

> Actually, it's a very easy role histrionically because he developed it so beautifully; I played her in the beginning of it as a kind of Marilyn Monroe type, a woman who is aware of the fact that men stop and look at her on the street and enjoys that but who's not in any way willfully evil. I don't think she set out to get Horace Tabor away from Augusta. I think, when she saw him, she did fall in love with him and he with her.

The "one difficulty," she reminisced, "that I had anticipated was that the ladies in the audience would be terribly sympathetic toward Augusta and not sympathetic toward Baby Doe."

Sills presented a delightful account in her book *Bubbles* (p. 84) of her audition for the role. Being told director Emerson Buckley thought she was too large physically for the part only spurred her on. By the time she arrived, over 100 sopranos had auditioned.

> I was being very defensive at that point, because I was
> irritated about being told that I was too large for something. I
> was simply not going to New York to be turned down. Then
> Emerson Buckley called me: Come on, come on in and
> audition. Buck, I said, there's no point if you think I'm too
> big for it. I won't be any smaller when I get to New York.
> "Get in here and sing," he said. Actually, he said something
> more vulgar than that. For the audition I wore the highest-
> heeled pair of new shoes I could find at Bergdorf's and a
> white mink hat of my mother's—I must have looked nine foot
> three. "Mr. Moore," I said to the composer, "this is how tall I
> am before I begin to sing for you and I'm going to be just as tall
> when I'm finished. We could save your time and my energy
> if you'd tell me now that I'm too big to play Baby Doe."

Moore wanted her to continue, which she did: "I sang the 'Willow Song.' Douglas walked down to the stage again and said, 'Miss Sills, you *are* Baby Doe.'"

In a March 2000 interview with David Kanzeg, Beverly again fondly recalled *Baby Doe* and Douglas Moore. She first met this "truly gentle, polite man" in the famous audition and too-tall episode. Before she sang, he came down the aisle and said, "Well, Miss Sills, you look just fine to me." She knew she had the job "when Emerson got up and started to conduct me. He slowed me down." Of the audition and role, Sills felt "it was a turning point in my career without question." She rated it her third-favorite role: "I loved Baby, I couldn't wait to play her. The nice thing about it, I was never finished with her. I could always find something new to do with her."

Sills provided insights into playing the role of Baby Doe. It was so important who sang Augusta, that was "my biggest challenge [because] every woman in the audience sympathized with her."

The biggest hurdle in playing Baby Doe "is not vocal, it's getting that female part of the audience to move over to her side—to understand that this was a great love and a great passion." The theme between the two women "is a killer." If you play her as a "slutty little gold digger to begin with, you are a dead duck." For Beverly, every character has a "line that describes her brilliantly, and for me 'live and let live is my motto' does it for Baby." She was not an "evil, slutty little girl who set her cap for Horace."

Looking back after forty years, Sills had not lost her enthusiasm for the opera or her feeling about who Baby was: "I just love her, really love her." The opera "is romantic and highly emotional. You can't be an intellectual singer and sing *The Ballad of Baby Doe*. You have to participate emotionally." Like others who sang the role of Baby, Sills felt the closing scene was an emotional experience. Beverly "used to weep every time Walter [Cassel] looked at me and sang 'you were always the real thing, Baby.' " She would say to herself "hold on," but she never "could divorce myself from that moment."

The opera "is so singable," the three roles "absolute dream roles." Yet "it is very difficult. There are challenges that can be so much fun to attempt to meet."

Speaking of the opera and the role, she explained in an earlier discussion, "You know it's a very long role to me. I've done five or six arias, and it's not an easy night in any way. The length of it is tremendous, and the dramatic scope of it is really rather enormous." After all this came the dramatic closing aria at the Tabor Grand and Matchless Mine: "It really is a very long, long drawn-out legato piece of singing, which is rather hard to do at the end of the night." This is Sills's favorite section of the opera: "I think it's the most beautiful piece of writing." And she concluded, "I think *The Ballad of Baby Doe* is a gorgeous opera."

Sills lived Baby Doe. Poignantly, she felt, it was "hard to say goodbye to Baby after each performance." Writing in *Bubbles* in 1976, she explained, "If I have ever achieved definitive performances during my career thus far, Baby Doe is one of them."

Although the audience probably never realizes it, sometimes a bit of humor creeps into the performance. This is true particularly if somebody in the cast has a sense of humor. Directors obviously frown on such "freelancing." Beverly recalled one such fleeting joke in the Washington wedding scene. The man playing President Chester Arthur was supposed to turn to her and say with astonishment, "Queen Isabella's jewels!" To her amusement, not to mention surprise, he sang, "Queen Isabella's Jewish?"

Chester Ludgin first appeared in *The Ballad of Baby Doe* in the 1958 New York City Opera production in the dual role as a saloon keeper and a Denver politician. During that time, he was also coached to sing the role of Tabor in case the scheduled performer was not available. He sang the same roles at Central City in 1959. Since then, he has sung Horace Tabor.

Ludgin highly praised Walter Cassel, who was generous in helping him learn the role: "He gave me all sorts of little insights that made my job a little easier. He inhabited the role so beautifully, and he was one of my inspirations. I like to think that Walter was one of my inspirations for knowing the degree of involvement you really have to have."

Baby Doe, in his estimation, has become an American classic. His first performance convinced him: "I thought it was a giant at the time because it made me feel so good to hear how all the dramatic situations were solved musically. It was just so perfect to my ears."

> I think it has an immediacy, especially for American ears, because it uses the vocabulary of some folk tunes here and there that just have a lilt that requires no deep intellectual penetration, except when the mood changes and it calls for that. Then Douglas Moore had the vocabulary to pull out all the stops and take you along with the music in his own way.

Moore received nothing but praise from Ludgin: "He was a remarkable composer. I can't say enough about him." After Latouche died, Moore wrote the "poker scene," which Chester feels "is one of the most exciting climaxes in the show. It's just great." Moore was a "mannerly guy. He was never brusque with anybody. He was very gentle." Moore heard Ludgin sing the role on various occasions, including Central City: "If he [Moore] made a correction at all, he would do it in such a way that it made you feel good. Moore would occasionally make people feel good about the amount of leeway that they would have because he didn't want a totally rigid musical performance when, instead, creating an atmosphere would do or it would be preferred." Moore inscribed on the title page of Ludgin's copy of *Baby Doe:* "To Chet with affection and great admiration of his Horace Tabor."

Ludgin sang opposite Beverly Sills, but not at Central City. "Beverly was so—I don't know whether she knows how supreme she was as Baby Doe. I did it with her several times as Tabor, and it was always a special event. The way she sang that damned thing in the final aria, and to hear how she holds on to that 'ever young syllable' for ever and ever and ever." Emerson Buckley "encouraged her to do that."

Ludgin always enjoyed Central City: "I did nine summers in Central City," performing in fourteen productions. Considering his busy schedule, it "would sort of restore my sanity for the rest of the year. I would sort of break the back of some of the music that I had to learn in the following year in Central City, but it was an outdoor existence, which I loved."

"Passionate" about the music is how Leyna Gabriele described her feelings toward the opera: "You see, it is an audience pleaser. The music is beautiful, the story is compelling, and the characters are interesting," and "people go and they respond to it." Having been with the opera from the very beginning, when she auditioned arias for Moore, through opening night, to seeing it performed in 1998–1999, Leyna concluded, "I think this is a story that grabs the hearts of the audience."

Frank Guarrera told a delightful story about his introduction to Central City in 1959. A jogger and athletically inclined, he was not worried about the altitude. He flew to Denver, rented a convertible, and drove up Clear Creek Canyon. "My heart started to pound" as he neared Central City, and then he arrived at the Teller House:

> I didn't bother opening the door. I simply jumped out of the car and ran up to the desk, and I was about to ask the man at the hotel desk if there was any mail for me. As I finished half of the sentence, I collapsed. He looked over the desk, and he

said, "You've got to remember that you are up pretty high here, and you can't be running around like that, young fellow."

The startled Guarrera "couldn't figure out what happened to me." Frank eventually did figure out what had happened, and he also learned a trick: "Some of us used to go up to an even higher altitude on the days we sang, mid-morning and so forth, and breathe some of that rarefied air. Then, coming back down, Central City was a little easier."

Frank studied "harder than anything" once he got the role of Horace. He even went so far as to order several boxes of cigars with "H.A.W. Tabor" written across the cigar band. Looking back at 1959 and his 1966 performance singing Tabor at Central City, he said, "It was really one of the most exciting experiences in my life," during a nineteen-year career. There is an "emotional excitement" in the role of Horace Tabor.

Highlights for him in *Baby Doe* included the scenes where Augusta found the gloves being sent to Baby Doe and the last act at the Tabor Grand Opera House, where Tabor asked Baby if he had failed her, too. In contrast, the happier opening scene, "smoking the cigar in the first act, when he knows Baby Doe is there" and Augusta calls to him to come up to their room, stands out in Guarrera's mind also: "Those are great moments in the theater for a person. I don't belittle all the other exciting things that happened on the stage, but these things sort of stay with you, and they are your little favorites."

The performers' appreciation for *Baby Doe* carried on through the years at Central City: "I want every opera house to do this opera. Everybody would love it. If those people could know how great it is, it would sell tickets because it's so Americana. I don't know why anybody wouldn't just fall in love with it. It's a love story. It couldn't be a more romantic love story." Thus did an enthusiastic Jan Grissom, the 1996 Central City Baby Doe, describe her "love affair" with the opera. "It's a very special role. It felt like they [Horace, Baby Doe, Augusta] kind of took you over. It was one of the most amazing performing experiences I've ever had, especially in Central City."

Regarding the role of Baby Doe, she said without hesitation, it "is absolutely my favorite role to sing."

> Not only because of the obvious reasons when you first look at it, but because of the many arias, which are just fabulous to sing. Some of them are more challenging than others, but it's the most romantic role. It's so genuine, it's so true. Then, when you do your research on it, you get pulled even more into the role and just all the people, all the characters.
>
> You get to see such a transition, from the very first moment she's on stage to the very last moment she's on stage. There's such growth for the character, and you don't always get to do that in roles, not to this extent. The time line is so nice—how they capture such a great amount and give you nice little scenes from each one.

Baby Doe "has such heart. I don't know of any other role that I do that has such heart, and [she] is so deeply, deeply in love with Tabor." The performer and the audience gain a sense of the inner Baby Doe. "She's so brave; at the same time, she's such a strong person. So you get to see how vulnerable she is through her heart and how strong she is, also, through her heart."

Jan, too, had trouble getting through the incredibly emotional last aria: "I don't know if John [Moriarty] told you, but in rehearsals I kept crying, and he was really afraid I wasn't going to make it through the performance. And I was the same way. I just couldn't quit crying. It caught me in my throat because of just being such an overwhelming scene, simply incredible." Finally, director Michael Ehrman suggested, "You are just going to have to try to turn this to thinking of the hopeful, positive." She did, and it worked.

Like others, she found the dryness more of a problem to her singing than the altitude: "Everybody said to drink Gatorade mixed with water, like half-and-half." Jan did notice the altitude, "but oh, it was so fun after you get used to it." She had one problem others did not have. The Opera Association does not allow pets in their housing—she had to find her own place to stay so she could have her two small dogs with her.

What is her opinion of the opera? From the previous comments, that should be obvious, but she went on to say:

I've heard people that don't think it's quite as well written as maybe some others, but I just love it so much. I'm not sure that I can be that objective because I think it's simply so much fun.

From a vocal standpoint, I love it. It's so much fun to sing. It's not so easy that you are bored with it; there's enough of a challenge to it. All the arias are just so—I love it. I think it's beautifully written.

Brian Steele, who has done six productions as Tabor—including 1988 and 1996 at Central City—made several points about the role of Horace: "It's very demanding. If he's not on stage, he's making a change, a quick change for the most part. Vocally, it's a challenge getting through the evening but especially not letting the emotion get to you, especially in that last scene." Brian once let the emotion take over: "I suddenly got a big catch in my throat, got very emotional about it, and realized that I couldn't do that. You can't get tied up emotionally because it ties you up vocally then, and I almost didn't make it through the rest of the act."

Discussing the three lead roles, Steele tipped his hat to Augusta: "I think actually Augusta is the best role. She almost always gets at least as good or better [a] reception than Horace. Everybody sympathizes" with her because "they feel she is the wronged woman, and, to a certain extent, she was." Baby Doe, on the other hand, proved the toughest character to get across to the audience. Why? "She is displayed in five very difficult arias, most of which are up in the stratosphere and most of which the audience can't understand, so they don't really know who she is."

Horace offers a great character to act and sing, although Brian hastened to add, "I don't say that I admire him. I think he was weak in many ways. He's a great character to portray on stage, and I enjoy very much doing it. He's got some great music to sing, and I would go anywhere to portray Horace. I really have a lot of fun with it. It's absolutely one of my favorite roles." "Warm as the Autumn" is his favorite aria. "Turn Tail and Run Then," also, is a "lot of fun, and you can get really emotional with that, of course."

Horace puffs on a cigar in the opening scene, a fact that does not bother Brian's singing. "I try to blow it off stage as much as I can" because it may bother others "if it gets too strong."

Like many fellow performers, he believes it takes awhile to adjust oneself to Central's elevation: "Not so much the singing of it, but getting rest. I know the first night or two I usually wake up several times during the night gasping for air. Until your body gets acclimated, that will happen. The dryness sometimes is actually more of a problem than the altitude, I think." Despite its coziness, the size of the opera house seems nearly perfect for *Baby Doe:* "That's what opera houses ought to be. You really ought to be where you can see the people, you need to see their faces." Opera "really is a very intimate art form," and one needs to be close to the people. The modest size of the stage is a "real drawback, there's no doubt about that." That is somewhat compensated for because of the history of the house, Brian felt. The association is "trying to keep it . . . much like it was for all those years." That is "the whole idea for having it in the first place."

Regarding a season at Central, Steele offered some interesting insights. "It's a good place to spend the summer, so you sort of think of it as a paid vacation." Besides, "it's a summer festival, and summer festivals are notoriously low paying. But you know, you have a lot of fun up there." Central is a "little teeny, tiny town. You do get to know a few of the local residents and become friends with them. Most of them that we do know also have ties to the opera."

Commenting on her role as his wife, Diane Steele simply said, "I'm just support." She attends performances and gets a little nervous, although she does not lack confidence in her husband. Brian added, "If I haven't been sleeping well because of the demand of the role, she doesn't know whether I'm going to bring it off or not."

Directing *Baby Doe* at Central provides challenges and joys, as Michael Ehrman explained during an interview. He has been involved in fourteen productions there, including *Baby Doe* in 1988 and 1996.

> Limitations to the stage space, that's the most obvious one. What's wonderful, and what is an advantage of the space, is the intimacy, which is also a challenge in terms of staging.
>
> Another thing is that there is limited wing space, and you don't have a lot of modern stage machinery on there.

Baby Doe presents its own special problems in its eleven different scenes.

> Every scene calls for a different set. In *Baby Doe* you've got
> eleven sets that are all very different locations, so you've got
> the challenge of fitting all the scenery on that stage. Getting
> from a scene, when there's not a lot of scene change music
> written for all those scenes, is tough. You've got a lot of people
> in the cast of *Baby Doe,* and it's tough to fit them all up there.

Another tricky aspect to the opera at Central City comes with
rehearsals. As Ehrman explained, there are "so many little sup-
porting parts and people running out for little vignettes that it's
tough to rehearse it." At Central, with its apprentice program,
"you have the five leads, and everybody else is in two other shows.
So you've got to try and coordinate getting people to the rehearsals and getting through scenes when you've got a lot of people to
keep track of that are also doing something else."

Changes have come to the opera. When Ehrman did the show
in 1988, "I used the original set design. It was very much a technique
of probably the pre-1960s theater. We used the old-fashioned technique, and it was built into the set where you ran the slide shows
in between scenes and both covered the set change, and it gave
you a real-life historic reference to the photographs." Then, in
1996, the new scenery appeared. "We went for a more contemporary way of going from scene to scene and left not so much the
flat painted drops as more scenery that had more dimension of
depth to it."

Ehrman loves *Baby Doe* for a variety of reasons. One is his
New York background, and the other is the challenges the opera
presents to the director.

> I think it's largely because I was raised on Broadway musicals,
> and to me *Baby Doe* is very close to a Broadway musical.
> Sure, the opening number, for example, "Right Here in
> Colorado," to me it's right out of *Paint Your Wagon.* It sounds
> like the score of *Paint Your Wagon* or the *Unsinkable Molly
> Brown.* Some of the choral music, like in the Bryan scene, has
> a real Broadway quality to it, I think. *Baby Doe* is what I
> would call old-fashioned in a sort of melodic, tuneful sense,
> which you associate with the musicals.

I think that there is a lot of variety to both the libretto and
the music. I find some of the challenges of it to be Baby
Doe's character itself. How to interpret her character,
because the libretto and score aren't totally specific and kind
of leave it up to the director and the singer's interpretation as
to just how much of a gold digger she was originally and was
she sincere from the very start.

From his research, he decided to interpret Baby Doe in this manner: she went to Leadville to meet the guy and "improve her fortune. Then, in the process, as she gets to know him, really falls
deeply and genuinely in love with him. That's the way I've gone
with it, because I think it makes it a more interesting story to see a
character that undergoes a change."

The "Willow Song" and "Warm as the Autumn Light" become key in developing Baby Doe's character.

I have her enter earlier than is indicated in the script. She
sees Horace is outside. That's why she sings the "Willow
Song," so that the "Willow Song" becomes in my interpretation more of a seduction aria.

You see her kind of manipulating him, but then during his
aria to her, "Warm as the Autumn Light," he kind of opens
his heart to her and becomes so vulnerable that he's partly
seducing her. But as the story goes on, they fall from what's
an infatuation (with her, more of an infatuation of the man's
position and money) to a real love.

Ehrman went on to discuss the type of person he wanted singing the role: "If you had a singer or an actress who had more of
a cold personality, it would be disastrous." He felt he had been
fortunate to have Baby Does who "have had strength but a soft-
ness and a charm."

As part of the challenge in developing her character, starting
her out a little bit more devious and manipulating, is that she
still has to have such charm.

So that while you watch Baby Doe doing this [flirting, then
having an affair with Horace], I don't think you really
disliked [her] or thought she was a terrible person. But there
is the element, for some people watching it, who might
consider her a home wrecker.

Yet there is another aspect to Baby Doe's part. She "sings so many arias, and somehow in some ways, even though she's the title character, she's the least fleshed out." Augusta "is the character that tends to win the audience over because, of course, the wronged wife is going to get sympathy."

Like others, the altitude and dryness concerned Myrna Paris, who sang the role of Mama McCourt in 1996. "I did have two vaporizers in my apartment, and the altitude, it only kept me from going out and doing a lot of walking, but it didn't bother me to sing there. I got acclimated."

She lived right across the street from the opera house. "I loved the opera house, a beautiful little gem." The smallness makes it "more intimate" with the audiences. Besides, being in Central City "was just fabulous, it was the best summer I've ever had. Part of it was the 40th anniversary and doing that opera, which I'd always wanted to do." Some of the enjoyment was "getting to know that little town and hanging out at the Teller House."

Central City "is really two towns, the gamblers below the Teller House and then the opera above that." During the interview, the question of gambling and its impact came up. Gambling changed the complexion of the town without doubt. Its effect on the opera was summarized by the observation, "Opera people will go and gamble, but gamblers never come to the opera."

Originally, Myrna auditioned for the role of Augusta for John Moriarty. She had been told he was "a rather formal man" and did not "want a lot of banter. So I was very restrained," sang a couple of arias, shook hands, "and left quietly." A month later he offered her the role of Mama McCourt. She asked him, "What in my personality that day showed you I could play that role?" "I could just tell," he replied, "and I read your résumé." Paris described why that choice may have been made: "I play a lot of kind of crazy, flamboyant character roles."

There was no question about her feelings toward John: "He's a wonderful man, and he helped me so much with the nuances of the score and everything." Like so many others, Paris observed about Moriarty and *Baby Doe,* "The opera is nearest and dearest to his heart."

She enjoyed the role of Mama and particularly praised the drama in Act II, Scene 4, where Mama confronts Augusta:

> I think it's just fabulous. It's very short in terms of actual measures to sing, but I think it's so well written. I love the wedding scene, it's a fun scene to do. But then I think the scene of her and Augusta in the second act is also really well-done. You will find very few scenes with just two mezzos in [them], and I always really enjoyed doing that scene with whoever was doing Augusta.

Regarding the opera, Paris admitted she had loved it since her college days: "It's just fascinating. It's not just the three leads, it's the little characters that are equally as well written and well drawn."

Dana Krueger sang the role of Augusta in 1981, 1988, and 1996 at Central City: "I think the character of Augusta is so well written. She's such an interesting and sympathetic character. And in a way, her music (I wouldn't say this to a Baby Doe's face) is more interesting. Augusta grows and changes, and it's a very sympathetic part." She always stands offstage, however, to hear Baby Doe's last aria, and "every damn show, when it starts to snow I start to cry."

Krueger respects all the Tabors as individuals and went on to say, "The characters are so human you can just see where they are going and how they got there, and it's a true tragedy in that sense. Everybody behaves pretty much as they have to behave. I mean, it's sort of Aristophanian in that way. They are all trapped."

When first asked to do the part of Augusta, Dana was concerned about Augusta's speech pattern: "I think a lot of what she sings, a lot of what she says in the opera reflects her changing station in life." Not knowing what a person from Maine might sound like, she turned to a friend from that state who "sort of taught me her Maine accent." Krueger sensed that Augusta's speech pattern would have changed when she got angry: "She uses the word *ain t*. She gets earthy and annoyed."

Considering the role of Augusta, Krueger pointed to several scenes that were particularly demanding to sing and act. Foremost was the finding of gloves for Baby Doe and the resulting fight with Horace; "that's one of the hardest things to play." Augusta gets so angry it "requires a great deal of restraint not to oversing that. You oversing it and you can't sing it all. It requires a great deal of craft, of just craftsmanship to feel that anger without its affecting your voice, because it can." If it does affect you, "then the audience loses the music, and you rob them through your own pleasure in wallowing in the emotion of the part. You rob the audience of the clarity of emotion. But it was very hard to play." A couple of times she came off the stage "practically sobbing" after the scene.

The Governor's Ball, she believes, ranks as the hardest scene. "Augusta says, 'Don't send me away,' and that's very difficult. It's emotionally difficult, very hard." Regarding the whole role, Dana found it "vocally difficult, but I think the hard part is that it's really emotionally difficult because there's so many parts to it. She goes through so many emotions." That is what makes Augusta so interesting and so sympathetic to the audience: "We see all sides of her, really, in some detail, even more than Horace, even more than Baby."

What are her feelings about *The Ballad of Baby Doe*? Dana Krueger sang its praises: "I love the show."

> I think it's one of the great shows. I really do. It's one of the great operas because the characters are so interesting and so human, the story is so touching, and the conflict between Horace and his wife is so plain and so straightforward and so complicated. It's just like any human relationship would be. You see how they got there, and you see that they sort of can't get out of it.

It takes a good conductor, Dana observed, because the music reflects "the emotions of the characters." A conductor can ruin it. "For example, in the very beginning we hear music . . . well, that's digging, for God's sake, what do you think that is. It's not just a tune, it's digging."

Central City offers an ideal place to produce *Baby Doe*. The small stage is not a handicap; quite the contrary. Dana Krueger saw it on a larger stage once: "The opera was lost on a great big stage because the characters are so immediate and so real. You want them in a confined space with the audience close so the audience can feel what the performers are feeling, what the characters are feeling."

At the close of an interview, she expressed a hope: "The more information that gets out about this wonderful opera, the better off we are all going to be. I want people to hear the opera and hear it for what it is." Amen!

EPILOGUE

I N HIS ARTICLE "The Great American Opera," David McKee made a strong argument for the readers of the *San Francisco Opera Magazine* (vol. 78, no. 3) that *The Ballad of Baby Doe* matched that standard. He laid down criteria for "trying to ascertain the identity of that wily and elusive critter known as the Great American Opera" and concluded:

> One work that meets the test with flying colors, one that has earned bragging rights to the Great American Opera sobriquet is Douglas Moore's *The Ballad of Baby Doe*. Despite its being one of the most-performed American operas (171 performances in Moore's [postopera] lifetime [1956–1969] including its premier season), *Baby Doe* is only now cracking the "big three" of American opera companies.

Christopher Hatch agrees. Writing in the *International Dictionary of Opera,* he calls for more regard for Moore as a composer: "When 20th-century modernism is being re-evaluated, Moore's operas, well-grounded in musical tradition and faithful to their national origin, deserve renewed respect." He went on to stress that "the very title of *The Ballad of Baby Doe* hints at the simplicity and reliance on convention that mark the work. Horace, Augusta, and Baby exemplify an archetypal love-triangle in the plainest way—a hero caught between women who represent respectively the power of love and the demands of social obligations." "For Moore," Hatch avowed, "the goal of being American transcended that of being modern."

Baby Doe captures an era and its people. The Tabors and their contemporaries could ask for no more. Nor could audiences past, present, and future who have the pleasure of spending a matinee or an evening with the Tabors and their friends in *The Ballad of Baby Doe.*

APPENDIX
Casts of Characters

1956

An old silver miner—Joseph Folmer, Howard Fried*, Alan Smith

A saloon bartender—Richard Wentworth

Horace Tabor, mayor of Leadville—Walter Cassel*, Clifford Harvuot

Jacob—James Duffin

Sam, Bushy, Barney, Bill, cronies and associates of Tabor—Joseph Folmer*, Howard Fried, Alan Smith*, James Duffin, John Miller, Edward Reams, Neil Webster

Augusta, wife of Horace Tabor—Frances Bible, Martha Lipton*

Mrs. Elizabeth (Baby) Doe, a miner's wife—Leyna Gabriele, Dolores Wilson*

Kate, Meg, dance hall entertainers—Marilyn Winters, Patricia Kavan

Samantha, a maid—Joyce Maiselsen

A clerk at the Clarendon Hotel—Joseph Folmer, Howard Fried, Alan
    Smith*

Albert, a bellboy—Richard Wentworth

Sarah, Mary, Emily, Effie, old friends of Augusta—Sylvia Anderson,
    Claire Jones, Cecelia Lomo, Judy Volkowitz

McCourt family—Eldon Breford, John Heiden, Patricia Kavan,
    Marilyn Winters

Mama McCourt, Baby Doe's mother—Beatrice Krebs

Four Washington dandies—Harrison Boughton, Stanley Burk,
    Michael Livingston, Donovan Wold

Father Chapelle, priest at the wedding—Joseph Folmer, Howard
    Fried*, Alan Smith

A footman at the Willard Hotel—Richard Wentworth

Chester A. Arthur, president of the United States—Joseph Folmer,
    Howard Fried, Alan Smith*

Elizabeth, Silver Dollar, children of Horace and Baby Doe Tabor—
    unknown

A Leadville dignitary—Joseph Folmer*, Howard Fried, Alan Smith

William Jennings Bryan, Democratic presidential candidate—
    Lawrence Davidson*, Norman Treigle

Stage doorman of the Tabor Grand Theatre—Joseph Folmer*,
    Howard Fried, Alan Smith

A Denver politician—Richard Wentworth

Silver Dollar (grown up)—Patricia Kavan

*Opening night cast
Musical Director: Emerson Buckley
Stage Directors: Hanya Holm, Edwin Levy

1959

An old silver miner—Grant Williams

A saloon bartender—Chester Ludgin

Horace Tabor, mayor of Leadville—Frank Guarrera, Clifford
    Harvuot

Sam, Bushy, Barney, Jacob, cronies and associates of Tabor—Joseph
    Folmer, Jack Harrold, William Kellogg, Osie Hawkins

Augusta, wife of Horace Tabor—Martha Lipton, Mary McMurray

Mrs. Elizabeth (Baby) Doe, miner's wife—Laurel Hurley, Judith Raskin

Kate, Meg, dance hall entertainers—Millie Fling, Lorraine Luck

Samantha, a maid—Brenda Bowyer

A clerk at the Clarendon Hotel—Joseph Folmer

Albert, a bellboy—Osie Hawkins

Sarah, Mary, Emily, Effie, old friends of Augusta—Barbara Rondelli, Martha O'Dell, Brenda Bowyer, Barbara Comstock

McCourt family—Millie Fling, Lorraine Luck, John Winn, William Kellogg

Mama McCourt, Baby Doe's mother—Ellen Repp

Four Washington dandies—David Dodds, Frank Tornabene, Dale Strong, Andrew Dirga

Father Chapelle, priest at the wedding—Grant Williams

A footman at the Willard Hotel—Osie Hawkins

Chester A. Arthur, president of the United States—Jack Harrold

Elizabeth, Silver Dollar, children of Horace and Baby Doe Tabor—Lynn Taussig, Jackie Haagenstad

Mayor of Leadville—James Kneebone

William Jennings Bryan, Democratic presidential candidate—Joshua Hecht

Stage doorman of the Tabor Grand Theatre—Grant Williams

A Denver politician—Chester Ludgin

Silver Dollar (grown up)—Lorraine Luck

1966

An old silver miner—Arthur Graham

A saloon bartender—Robert Falk, James Fleetwood

Horace Tabor, mayor of Leadville—Frank Guarrera, Chester Ludgin

Sam, Bushy, Barney, Jacob, cronies and associates of Tabor—Michael Devlin, Thomas Palmer, Anthony Morton, Philip Lehmberg

Augusta, wife of Horace Tabor—Frances Bible, Eunice Alberts

Mrs. Elizabeth (Baby) Doe, miner's wife—Lucille Kailer, Nadja Witkowska

Kate, Meg, dance hall entertainers—Karen Pomplun, Doris Peterson

Samantha, a maid—Doris Peterson

A clerk at the Clarendon Hotel—Leo Goeke

Albert, a bellboy—Robert Falk, James Fleetwood

Sarah, Mary, Emily, Effie, old friends of Augusta—Patricia Imel, Marlene Mayland, Norma Sharp, Carol Wilcox

McCourt family—Doris Peterson, Karen Pomplun, James Simmerman, Dennis Wadsworth

Mama McCourt, Baby Doe's mother—Beatrice Krebs

Four Washington dandies—Donald Canady, Paul Nutt, Robert Seeley, Michael Warren

Father Chapelle, priest at the wedding—Leo Goeke

A footman at the Willard Hotel—Robert Falk, James Fleetwood

Chester A. Arthur, president of the United States—Arthur Graham

Elizabeth, Silver Dollar, children of Horace and Baby Doe Tabor—Carol Hayward, Linda Hayward

Mayor of Leadville—Leo Goeke

William Jennings Bryan, Democratic presidential candidate—Herbert Beattie, Lee Cass

Stage doorman of the Tabor Grand Theatre—Arthur Graham

A Denver politician—Robert Falk, James Fleetwood

Silver Dollar (grown up)—Doris Peterson

1976

An old silver miner—Ellis Acker

A saloon bartender—Carlos Serrano

Horace Tabor, mayor of Leadville—Frederick Burchinal, Adib Fazah

Sam, Bushy, Barney, Jacob, cronies and associates of Tabor—Michael Myers, Joseph Wilson, Robert Lyon, Robert Hussa

Kate, Meg, dance hall entertainers—Kristine Ciesinski, Martha Toney

Augusta, wife of Horace Tabor—Muriel Costa-Greenspon, Margaret Yauger

Mrs. Elizabeth (Baby) Doe, a miner's wife—Gianna Rolandi, Paula Seibel

Sarah, Mary, Emily, Effie, old friends of Augusta—Madeleine Mines, Monica Robinson, Ellen Grogan, Betsy Hoover

Cousin Jack—Bruce Hanson

Samantha, a maid—Martha Toney

A clerk at the Clarendon Hotel—Joseph Wilson

Albert, a bellboy—Carlos Serrano

Mama McCourt, Baby Doe's mother—Sharon Abel, Kathryne Fowler

Four Washington dandies—Michael Myers, Joseph Wilson, Carlos Serrano, Michael Burt

McCourt family—Kryste Johnsen, Gary Jordan, Cindy Sheppard, Marc Soto

Father Chapelle, priest at the wedding—Ellis Acker

A footman at the Willard Hotel—David Austin

A waiter—Charles Emery

Chester A. Arthur, president of the United States—Jonathan Green

Elizabeth, Silver Dollar, children of Horace and Baby Doe Tabor— Arlette Aslanian, Christina Mason, Nicole Burchinal, Juanita Pisano, Hilary Trampler

Mayor of Leadville—Joseph Wilson

William Jennings Bryan, Democratic presidential candidate— Herbert Eckhoff, Malcolm Smith

Stage doorman of the Tabor Grand Theatre—Ellis Acker

A Denver politician—Michael Burt

Silver Dollar (grown up)—Martha Toney

1981

An old silver miner—Samuel L. Cook

A saloon bartender—William D. Parcher

Horace Tabor—William Justus

Sam—Christopher Critelli

Bushy—Frank Farina

Barney—David Neal

Jacob—Curt Scheib

Katie—Jean Glennon

Meg—Jean Cantrell

Augusta Tabor—Dana Krueger

Sarah—Ruthann Turekian

Mary—Randy Minkin
Emily—Lynn Yakes
Effie—Judy Donham
Mrs. Elizabeth Doe, known as "Baby"—Karen Hunt
Samantha—Lisa Monheit
A clerk at the Clarendon Hotel—Kim Scown
Albert, a bellboy—David Orcutt
Mama McCourt, Baby Doe's mother—Jocelyn Wilkes
Washington dandies—Samuel L. Cook, Richard Blocher, James
    McGuire, William D. Parcher
Cornelia McCourt—Jean Cantrell
Claudia McCourt—Joan Campbell
Peter McCourt—John McGhee
Phillip McCourt—Ken Peterson
Papa McCourt—David Orcutt
Father Chapelle—Kim Scown
A footman at the Willard Hotel—Steven Taylor
Elizabeth Tabor, age 12—Jane Cady, Krista Waldmann
Silver Dollar (as a child)—Karina Steele, Holly Byerly
Chester A. Arthur, president of the United States—Frank Farina
Mayor of Leadville—Richard Blocher
William Jennings Bryan—Brian Robertson
Newsboys—Christopher Critelli, Richard Blocher
Doorman at the Tabor Grand—Richard Blocher
A Denver politician—Brian Robertson
Silver Dollar (grown up)—Joan Lauren Campbell
Saloon girls, miners, wedding guests, ambassadors and their wives,
    sailors—apprentice artists, studio singers, and performing
    ensemble

1988

An old miner—Joseph Myering
Bartender—Robert Holden
Kate, a dance hall entertainer—Deborah Cole
Meg, a dance hall entertainer—Annette Daniels

Horace A.W. Tabor, mayor of Leadville—Brian Steele

Cronies and associates of Tabor: Bushy, Sam, Barney, Jacob—Frank
    Levar, Jeff Martin, Mark Gargiulo, Joseph Oechsli

Augusta Pierce Tabor, Mrs. H.A.W. Tabor—Dana Krueger

Friends of Augusta: Sarah, Mary, Emily, Effie—Debrah Ehrhardt*,
    Susan Owen[†], Heidi Hayes, Lee Staff, Kathryn Garber

Mrs. Elizabeth Doe, known as "Baby Doe"—Amy Burton

Samantha, Augusta's maid—Susan Owen*, Debrah Ehrhardt[†]

A clerk at the Clarendon Hotel—Dean Anthony

Albert, a bellboy—Barry Johnson

Mama McCourt, Baby Doe's mother—Jayne Sleder

State Department Dandies—Curt Peterson, Robert Chafin, David
    Kravitz, Rod Nelman

Father Chapell, priest at the wedding—Dean Anthony

A footman—Barry Johnson

Chester A. Arthur, president of the United States—Joseph Myering

Lillie Tabor—Sarah Martin

Silver Dollar, as a child—Ashley Holden

Mayor of Leadville, 1896—Joseph Myering

William Jennings Bryan, candidate for president—Henry Kiichli

Newsboys—Robert Chafin, Curt Peterson

Stage doorman of the Tabor Grand—Dean Anthony

A Denver politician—Robert Holden

Silver Dollar, grown up—Annette Daniels

Saloon girls, miners, wedding guests, ambassadors and their wives—
    apprentice and studio artists

*first seven performances
[†]last seven performances

1996

An old miner—Torrance Blaisdell

Bartender—Jeffrey McCollum

Kate, a dance hall entertainer—Becky Budd

Meg, a dance hall entertainer—Jessie Raven

Horace A.W. Tabor, mayor of Leadville—Brian Steele

Cronies and associates of Tabor: Bushy, Sam, Barney, Jacob—Eric
    Erik, Theodore Green, James Taylor, Mark Freiman

Augusta Pierce Tabor, Mrs. H.A.W. Tabor—Dana Krueger

Friends of Augusta: Sarah, Mary, Emily, Effie—Brigitte Bellini,
    Gwendolyn Coleman, Lindarae Polaha, Monica Bellner

Mrs. Elizabeth Doe, known as "Baby Doe"—Jan Grissom

Samantha, Augusta's maid—Juline Barol

A clerk at the Clarendon Hotel—Vale Rideout

Albert, a bellboy—Curtis Olds

Mama McCourt, Baby Doe's mother—Myrna Paris

State Department dandies—Erik Lautier, Steven Veguilla, Andrew
    Krikawa, Paul Ivan

Father Chapelle, priest at the wedding—Vale Rideout

A footman—Curtis Olds

Chester A. Arthur, president of the United States—Torrance Blaisdell

Lillie Tabor—Joanna Miano, Briana Selstad

Silver Dollar, as a child—Jacquelyn Billings, Janay Hagen

Mayor of Leadville, 1896—Torrance Blaisdell

William Jennings Bryan, candidate for president—George Hogan,
    Mark Freiman

Newsboys—Erik Lautier, Steven Veguilla

Stage doorman of the Tabor Grand—Vale Rideout

Denver politician—Paul Bellantoni

Silver Dollar, grown up—Kathryn Honan-Carter

Saloon girls, miners, wedding guests—apprentice and studio artists

Ambassadors—Lew Cady, Richard Evans, Carl Mees

FOR ADDITIONAL INFORMATION ON
THE BALLAD OF BABY DOE

———◦◦◦◦———

THOSE WHO WISH TO GO FURTHER into the stories of the Tabors, the Opera Association, and the opera itself will find original materials, books, and a variety of publications available. If you are interested in primary sources, the Colorado Historical Society, Denver University Archives, and the Denver Public Library Western History/ Genealogy Department provide places to start. Denver and New York newspapers and a variety of magazines provide reviews of the premier season and, to a lesser degree, of the *Baby Doe* seasons that follow. For up-to-date coming performances and a variety of information, check the *Baby Doe* website: www.babydoe.org.

The place of *Baby Doe* in American opera is examined in the following: Gilbert Chase, *America s Music: From the Pilgrims to the*

Present (Urbana: University of Illinois Press, 1988 ed.); *"The Ballad of Baby Doe," International Dictionary of Opera* (Detroit: St. James, 1993); and David McKee, "The Great American Opera?" *San Francisco Opera Magazine* (78, no. 3), 10–18. The programs for the seven productions of *Baby Doe* at Central City are also informative about the opera, the opera house, and the Tabors. Beverly Sills discusses the opera and her part in it in two books: Beverly Sills and Lawrence Linderman, *Beverly* (New York: Bantam, 1987), and Beverly Sills, *Bubbles* (New York: Bobbs-Merrill, 1976).

The Central City Opera House Association and its role in the opera are found in Charles A. Johnson, *Opera in the Rockies* (Denver: Central City Opera House Association, 1992), and Allen Young, *Opera in Central City* (Denver: Spectrographics, 1993). Randie Lee Blooding, "Douglas Moore's *The Ballad of Baby Doe*" (unpublished M.A. thesis, Ohio State University, 1979), has a few gems that can be found nowhere else.

The Tabors have received a great deal of attention in pamphlets and books. In fact, they are the best-known nineteenth-century Coloradans. Lewis Gandy, *The Tabors* (New York: Press of the Pioneers, 1934), Betty Moynihan, *Augusta Tabor* (Evergreen: Cordillera, 1988), and Duane A. Smith, *Horace Tabor: His Life and the Legend* (Niwot: University Press of Colorado, 1989) present a starting point. So do the various publications of the Colorado Historical Society, which offer a variety of Tabor articles.

INDEX